THE 12 KEYS TO FEELING GOOD (ALL THE TIME)

THE 12 KEYS TO FEELING GOOD (ALL THE TIME)

Liz Adamson

iUniverse, Inc.
New York Lincoln Shanghai

THE 12 KEYS TO FEELING GOOD (ALL THE TIME)

Copyright © 2005 by Liz Adamson

All rights reserved. No part of this book may be used or reproduced by any means, graphic, electronic, or mechanical, including photocopying, recording, taping or by any information storage retrieval system without the written permission of the publisher except in the case of brief quotations embodied in critical articles and reviews.

iUniverse books may be ordered through booksellers or by contacting:

iUniverse
2021 Pine Lake Road, Suite 100
Lincoln, NE 68512
www.iuniverse.com
1-800-Authors (1-800-288-4677)

ISBN-13: 978-0-595-37316-1 (pbk)
ISBN-13: 978-0-595-81713-9 (ebk)
ISBN-10: 0-595-37316-X (pbk)
ISBN-10: 0-595-81713-0 (ebk)

Printed in the United States of America

Contents

INTRODUCTION 1
KEY ONE CLEAR THE CLUTTER. 7
KEY TWO LET THE PAST GO. 15
KEY THREE STAY IN THE PRESENT. 27
KEY FOUR MAKE GOOD INVESTMENTS 38
KEY FIVE BROADEN YOUR HORIZONS 49
KEY SIX BE CREATIVE 60
KEY SEVEN LIVE LIFE ON PURPOSE 67
KEY EIGHT HARMONISE YOUR ENVIRONMENT. 78
KEY NINE BE KIND 87
KEY TEN HAVE FUN 96
KEY ELEVEN TAKE TIME FOR YOURSELF 102
KEY TWELVE GRATITUDE. 109
FINAL NOTE 115

INTRODUCTION

The whole of my life and work is dedicated to helping myself and others to find and reach their highest potential and optimal lives. The means by which I do this is through my unique brand of therapy that clears all the things that get in the way of living life to the full. I have written twelve personal growth books so far, on subjects such as relationships, abundance, abuse, weight, releasing anger, fear, guilt and pain. Each book is designed to provide the reader with an understanding of the subject and the practical means by which the prevalent issues and patterns may be released. I am the founder of the Institute of Optimal Living which provides workshops and training for therapists in the Adamson Technique.

My philosophy is to make things as simple and accessible as possible in order to achieve the greatest transformation for the greatest number of people. This philosophy is no less true for the *Twelve Keys to Feeling Good*. All of the keys are known to us on an intellectual or theoretical level but the gap between knowing and doing is enormous. This is a handbook for living that gives an understanding of what makes us feel good and also the means by which we can either clear the blocks or consciously bring in what is needed.

Each of these keys has been personally tested by me and I was amazed to discover how energized, productive, happy and at peace I became as a result of putting them in *action*. There became a synchronicity in my life that I had only previously experienced in fleeting patches. I realized that the means to create this is now in my full power and control. Whenever my life feels like it is getting bogged down, I have only to look at which keys I need to reinforce or clear the blocks. For instance, I may have to clear some outstanding business and bring myself back into the moment.

Most of us are motivated by our need to feel good. Yet the means that we use to find that feel good factor are failing us and, in many cases, take us further away from where we want to be.

There is no doubt about it: we are living in a material world and we are bombarded by propaganda that wants us to think that things will make us feel good. Never have we had such spending power and yet the instances of stress and depression are also at an all time high. More people visit the doctor for depression than for any other ailment including colds, flu and back problems.

When we buy or are given things, there may be a moment of pleasure but it is usually very quick to subside. Often the anticipation of the things we are going to get is better than the reality. Shopping addiction is very common. These addicts use shopping and things to try and make up for a sense of lack and deprivation. They will get a buzz or high while they are shopping but this will usually be followed by guilt and a huge low. Many shopaholics never even open or use the things that they buy.

Over-consumption is one of the big problems in the Western world. I put this down to the need to feel good and the illusion that things will provide it. Not only do we have more things than we could possibly need, but there are not enough hours in the day to listen to all the CDs, watch all the videos or read all the books that we buy.

When we are looking for what will make us feel good, we have to weigh it up with any possible negative consequences that arise from having or using these things. It is no good going back to the things that may give us five minutes of pleasure but hours of guilt, fear or self-disgust.

Food is one thing that most people will look to to help them feel good. The consequence of this is that the West is currently suffering an epidemic of obesity. Most of the foods that we turn to for pleasure are also the ones that will put on weight and do not nurture our inner selves.

Food is no longer about nutrition; for many people it is about comfort, companionship, de-stressing and pleasure. Like anything else that is external, the good feeling is short lived. If we use sugar to give us a lift, we will get an initial boost but this will soon result in our going further back down than when we started. We will then look to have more and more to give us the same lift.

Alcohol is another substance that we use to make us feel good. Once again, we need to look at the long term effects here. One or two drinks may relax us, lift our spirits and help us to feel better but more than that will actually create the opposite effect. Alcohol is actually a depressant and not a stimulant. The other downside of using alcohol to feel good is that the resulting hangover the next day feels anything but good.

Drugs are often used in an attempt to feel better. This is, of course, a total illusion. Even the drug Ecstasy promises that we will feel good as a result of having taken it. The trouble is that when first taking drugs there will be a huge high and feel good factor. It will block out the issues, problems and feelings that we want to run away from. The effect is short lived and very soon the drugs are only there to ward off the dreadful feeling of withdrawal. Even prescription drugs designed to combat the effects of depression and anxiety do not give us the feel good factor. Prozac was once dubbed "the happy pill." This is not the reality. Antidepressants will often dull or numb the feelings and while this may reduce the negative feelings, it will also numb the positive ones. Rather than feeling good, we just don't feel at all.

Many of us look to other people to make us feel good. This is most common in the arena of relationships. In the early stages of a relationship we give away our power to our partner in return for the understanding that they will make us happy. The fact is that when we give someone the power to make us happy, we also give them the power to make us unhappy. As with every other means that we use to make us feel good, the effects are only in the short term. Ultimately, the only reason why a relationship breaks up is because one or both partners no longer feel good in it. We have only to see the divorce rate to know that relationships are not making us feel good and this is only the tip of the iceberg. Many relationships that do not break up are far from happy.

All the means by which we are in the main using to make us feel good are external and the effects are fleeting and short-lived. This sets up needing more and more of the thing to keep on getting the pleasure or buzz that we do from it. In the long term there are often very destructive consequences to our pursuit of the feel good factor. We therefore have to look elsewhere for what genuinely can make us feel good.

The criteria for feeling good is first and foremost that it must be within our own power and control. This means that we are not dependant on people, things or substances to give us the feeling and we therefore cannot be let down or disappointed by them. We also have to feel worthy and deserving of feeling good or we won't take the steps to achieve it. This is a huge issue for many people. They spend their lives punishing, sabotaging or depriving themselves and would be unlikely to choose to feel good.

We also need to ensure the good feeling is long term and ongoing. Indeed, it is a matter of continually raising our energy and seeing it have a positive knock on effect into various areas of our lives as well as to the people that we have in our lives.

Feeling good is an internal quality and consequently it is never going to be enough to try and achieve it through purely external means. The feel good factor that I am referring to in this book is so much more than just happiness. I don't think there is a word in our vocabulary that suitably describes this feeling, which probably goes to show how little it is actually experienced. The feeling involves inner peace and contentment at the same time as joy, enthusiasm, fulfilment, satisfaction and raised energy levels. We feel powerful and as if everything is possible.

At our highest level our common goal and purpose is to achieve Heaven on Earth. Sadly, the majority of people are probably closer to creating Hell on Earth. It is totally within our own choice and power as to which state we end up manifesting. In this book my intention is to give guidance and tips to help readers to create the Heaven and the feel good factor that goes with it.

The twelve keys to feeling good is an ongoing process and it is up to each individual as to how much time and effort he or she is willing to devote to feeling good. What I will guarantee is that with each change and shift that takes place, you will find that your feel good quotient will go up. How far can it go? The sky is the limit. I don't think that we have even begun to experience the heights that we could reach.

Ultimately, the reason why these keys work is because they either free up or raise the vibration of our inner energy. If we are to put it in a nutshell, what we are meant to be doing here, is to raise our energy vibration. Every time we succeed in doing this, we will feel better and better.

The biggest block there is to raising our energy to higher levels is fear. Many of the steps involve letting go and removing fear from our lives. The more fear we have, the worse we will feel and the less our lives will function in an optimal way.

Some of the keys involve doing practical, active things in your life, while others involve an inner change in your attitude or patterns. Any changes that take place either internally or externally will need to be reinforced until they are integrated into your normal patterns. It takes determination and discipline to do this but the rewards will make it well worth it. I would recommend that you make life as easy as possible for yourself and start with the keys that are less of a challenge and work up to the more difficult ones.

KEY ONE
CLEAR THE CLUTTER

*Clearing clutter pares our
lives down to what is
useful, beautiful or enhances
our existence.*

CLEAR THE CLUTTER

I have chosen to put clear the clutter as the first of the twelve keys because it was this that inspired me to write this book. I have been a devotee of clutter-clearing for many years. I find that stuff tends to build up and then I have a phase of chucking out and reassessing what my current needs are. I have noticed time and again over the years that whenever I clear out old stuff and streamline my living space, there is always a huge knock-on effect in my life. I may become more productive or get new inspiration that propels my life forward and I seem to have extra energy to put things into action.

On this particular occasion I had been clearing out for about a week and suddenly there was nowhere that was still clogged with stuff; my bills were paid and my desk was clear. I noticed how good I felt as a result of this and the raised energy levels meant that I was looking for my next project to channel the energy into. I felt a massive high that was not as a result of any external substance or reliant on any other person. This got me thinking about all the things in life that provide this feel good factor and are in our power and control to create. The rest is history.

Clearing our clutter works on many levels. There is clutter that can be seen, there is clutter that is tangible but hidden out of sight and then there is internal clutter that is known only to ourselves but will have a hugely detrimental effect on our lives.

Everything in life is made up of energy and energy is meant to flow, not stagnate. When we have too much stuff, it bogs us down and slows down the energy flow in our lives and homes. Clearing the stuff away will allow the energy to flow once more.

First I am going to address clutter that is visible in the home. If we have surfaces that are packed with knick-knacks or papers, magazines and the bits and pieces of daily life, these things will gather dust and block energy. If we have lots of ornaments, we will have to spend a great deal of time dusting and maintaining them. Even worse is when they are not cleaned and dusted and are allowed to fester.

Sentimentality is often at the root of our need to hold on to all the bits and pieces that we have around. They may be presents received or a child's pottery ashtray made at school. In clearing this sort of clutter, you don't have to throw everything out. You could keep a memory box or trunk where these things are kept or you could recycle things every few months giving different pieces pride of place.

I know for myself that whenever I go into a person's house where there are too many things around, I feel very uncomfortable and will often end up with a headache. I certainly breathe a sigh of relief when I leave. Usually there are some beautiful things there that are completely lost and swamped by all the other things. I have also noticed that the people who live in all the clutter are often very stuck in their lives. It is certainly a symptom.

There are many psychological reasons why people are hoarders or collectors and these may need to be addressed before there will be a willingness to let go. Fear and the need for security will always be at the core of these reasons. It may be a fear of lack or deprivation and the things represent a buffer between them and any circumstances that may occur in the future. Some people who have experienced poverty and hunger in the past may fill their cupboards with food and keep on buying more instead of using up what is there. This gives them a sense of security and it is hard to break the association.

In clearing the visible clutter, it is a good idea to start with things like papers, magazines and books. There may be resistance to this, as for many people knowledge is power and the information contained in the written material represents having this knowledge at their finger tips and available if they should need it. The fact is that we rarely if ever dip into the information and usually forget that we have it anyway. We can get into the habit of clearing our papers on a daily basis and not keeping any periodical past the month it covers. If we have read a book and will not want to read it again, it needs to be passed on or given to a charity shop.

Work up to the more permanent things around your home. Be honest with yourself as to whether there is too much stuff. There is a fine balance between too much and not enough. The trick is to strike that balance. You will know when you have hit it because the energy in the room will transform. A minimalist approach can be as bad as too much clutter. Without imprinting our taste and personality, the atmosphere can be cold, sterile and unwelcoming.

When clearing your bits and pieces, you need to have a scale of 1-10 of either usefulness or attractiveness. Never keep anything that is below a five and try to have only sevens to tens in your home. If something has sentimental value and you can't bear to part with it, find an unobtrusive place for it.

Once the visible clutter is dealt with, it is time to deal with the hidden clutter. This is the stuff in the drawers, cupboards, lofts or garages. There may be more resistance to doing this. If we understand that our outer environment is a reflection of our external physical selves, the visible clutter is going to reflect what we show to the world. Clearing our visible clutter is the equivalent of making over our hair, clothes and make-up. Going in and clearing the hidden stuff represents letting go from our inner or unconscious selves and it may seem harder to go there.

Our hidden clutter will include things like papers, bills, receipts and out of date warranties and instruction books. Only keep what is current or needed for records. It is also a good idea to go through things like photographs and only keep the good ones and perhaps put them in an album where you will look and enjoy them more. It is also very satisfying clearing out ill fitting, unworn or old clothes. Often we buy clothes that do not fit or we don't feel comfortable in. We fool ourselves that we will lose weight or there will be some miracle that will enable us to wear them. If it doesn't fit or you don't wear it, chuck it. Women may also need to go through cosmetics and beauty products that will be out of date or no longer used.

Paying bills and getting all our paperwork up to date is a very important aspect of clearing our clutter. When these things are left to hang over us, they waste a huge amount of energy. If we have let these things go for too long, they can almost paralyse us. We feel incapable of going near it and we find any excuse to avoid tackling this monster. It may help to put aside time to do these and plan a reward for yourself when you have done this.

Clearing the clutter can become a very addictive activity. However, as addictions go this is a good one. There is such a sense of satisfaction and a huge high that goes with letting stuff go. Once the high begins to wear off, we look for more things to clear and get the feeling back. The knock on positive effect is that we have a great deal more energy to spend in our lives. We follow the same laws of energy that many of us learned in physics. Nature abhors a vacuum. When we make space, we leave room for something new to come in. This is why things tend to happen and shift in our lives after we have done some clutter clearing. If you are someone who feels that nothing much happens in your life or things are very stuck or stagnant, then this should be a sign to do some clutter clearing.

There is another side benefit that often comes with letting our stuff go. Many people find that they lose weight. This makes sense as we are releasing our excess baggage on an outer level which shows that we are willing to let go of our physical extra baggage. The added energy we get as a result of clearing can often be used to motivate us into making other changes in our lives. I have often noticed that some people with a weight issue will also hang on to stuff or have the need to keep acquiring more and more stuff that fills their homes to the brim. Once again this will be an outer reflection of our inner issues.

Another huge advantage to clearing physical clutter is that you can use it to generate another form of energy, money. One man's junk is another man's treasure. Car boot sales or auctions can be quite lucrative. This will be particularly true if you have been a collector in the past. Even if you do not choose to use your clutter to raise money for yourself, you could use it to benefit others by giving it to a charity shop or bazaar. Even old books and clothes would be welcome there.

It is not just in the home that we need to practice clutter clearing. We can extend it to the work place. This can mean that we let go of unworkable practices, clear out old paperwork or let go of clients, workers or products that do not provide us with what we need. Clearing out the dead wood will make space for new work or business to come in and generate more money and energy.

We also need to extend the principle of clutter clearing to areas of life other than just the material. The premise that we are using in clutter clearing is that we are letting go of the things that we do not need, do not enhance our lives in any way and are taking up space and blocking the flow of energy. If we put the same understanding to the people in our lives, there may well be friends, acquaintances or associates that have passed their sell-by dates. We will often outgrow our friends or will no longer be involved with the areas that we once had in common. Some friends may be professional users, taking what we have to offer and giving nothing back in return. It may be necessary to look at the people that we have in our lives and if any of them drain us, use us, make us feel bad about ourselves or are a chore to be with, it may be time to clear them from our lives. This culling process does not need to be painful or confrontational to either you or them. It will be a question of withdrawing energy from the friendship until it eventually fades and dies. Once again, the advantage of doing this is that we free up a great deal of energy and we make space for new, more positive people to come into our lives.

We may also need to remove the clutter from our minds. If we are very busy or have a lot going on in our lives, it may result in a very busy brain that can almost drive us demented. To remove this brain-clutter we need to get organised. The first step for this is to put the things going round and round the brain onto paper. The mind knows that when the information is down in black and white, it can let the thoughts go and make room for other things. Make sure that all the things that need doing are prioritised and scheduled into your life. Only focus on the next thing on the list. The other stuff will be dealt with when the time is right. It does not need any thought until then. It may be that if you are constantly stressed or overloaded, you need to let go of some areas of life that do not give satisfaction and fulfilment.

Tips For Clearing Clutter

1) Look at the scale of the clutter you have in you home, work and life.

2) Note whether there is any resistance to letting it go. If the clutter is extensive, it may seem very overwhelming and it may seem easier to stick your head in the sand.
3) Make the decision to start the process and put some time aside to do it.
4) If this is a big issue for you, get some help or support. Get a friend or relative to help you.
5) Make the process as pleasurable as possible. Put on some music or open a bottle of wine.
6) Be ruthless. If you do not need these things in your life now, then get rid of them. Do not be fooled into thinking that it may be needed or useful at some time in the future.
7) Remember the criteria. Only keep things that you need, enhance your life or give you pleasure.
8) Sort the stuff into piles. Throw away, give away or sell at a car boot sale or auction.
9) Start with the visible clutter in the rooms that you use most. If it is a big job, start with one corner or shelf. You will find that it is so satisfying that you will be inspired to do some more.
10) Make sure that this does not become an exercise in moving clutter from one place to another.
11) Work through your home as time and inclination allow.
12) Clear out old papers, receipts, bank statements etc.
13) Make sure all your paperwork and bills are up to date.
14) Look at how you can let clutter go from your workplace and generate new energy there.
15) Look at the people you have in your life that detract rather than enhance it. Start to let them go by breaking the patterns and the ways that you interact. It may take a while to do this but keep withdrawing the time and energy you devote to them. This will make the final release much easier.
16) Look at the things you have on your plate. Do you find that you are overextended? If so, organise and prioritise and let go of anything that does not serve you.

17) Make sure you do not let clutter build up again. Use the criteria for removing clutter when you are tempted to buy more things. Ask yourself if you need it, if it will make your life easier or will it add beauty or enhance your environment.

18) Notice the difference in how you feel when you clear both internal and external clutter. Use the boost of energy to do productive things so that you can increase the feel-good effect.

KEY TWO
LET THE PAST GO

Release the limiting patterns, beliefs and emotions that have come from past experiences. Create each new moment with a clear canvas to be what you want.

LET THE PAST GO

I believe that one of the main reasons why many people find it difficult to enjoy all the good fortune and potential that they have is because they are carrying issues and emotions from the past into their current lives. I am always seeing clients who in reality have a wonderful life with all the boxes ticked and yet they find it hard to be happy and take advantage of what they have.

Clearing from the past is the next key on from clutter clearing because in a way it is the same process on a deep inner level. It is about assessing if we still want to carry the rubbish from the past that we are holding onto and if not, we have to throw it out. We have to decide what we still need and will enhance our lives and let go of the rest.

Letting the past go is certainly easier said than done. Most of us have no idea how we go about processing and moving on from our past experiences. I will endeavour to explain what we carry from the past and how to move on from it so that we can create the future that we want for ourselves.

There are three things that we tend to hold onto from the past: emotions, patterns of behaviour and beliefs. Each of these impact us in different ways but will often have a very detrimental effect on our lives. I will address each of these separately and help uncover how they work in our lives.

Most of the issues and stuff from the past is carried in our unconscious selves. This means that we may not be conscious or aware of what we are carrying but it will certainly be impacting on us. For some people it seems like there is a black cloud that follows them around. We don't feel good but we don't know why. Many people go through life with mild depression and actually think that this is normal because they have never known any different.

Negative emotions are the biggest block to our feeling good. We often term it emotional baggage and this is a very good analogy. If we are carrying a great deal of emotional baggage from the past, it will weigh us down, sometimes to the extent that we are totally unable to move forward.

If we can imagine what it would be like to carry ten heavy suitcases with us wherever we go. Very soon we would choose not to go anywhere because the hassle of lugging this stuff with us is too much. This is exactly how the emotional baggage affects us but in a non-tangible way. Emotions will bog us down and prevent us from flowing and moving forward in our lives.

There are four main emotions that have a particularly detrimental effect on us. These are fear, anger, hurt and guilt. Each one will have a different cause and application. One thing is a certainty: it is virtually impossible to feel good when we are feeling any of these four emotions. They drag us down and colour every aspect of our lives and living. I will look at each of these feelings individually.

Fear is always going to be the predominant block to feeling good. It will be at the core of every negative situation, feeling and behaviour that there is in the world. My definition of fear is that it is a projection into the future about something that has already happened in the past. This is a classic case of carrying our past baggage with us.

The common manifestations of fear are worry, doubt, panic and anxiety. We can all associate with some of these. Worry is probably the biggest of these. We are constantly projecting all sorts of negative situations into our future and feeling them as if they were already happening now. It is almost impossible to feel good when we are in a constant state of worry.

Worry is a pattern and habit that we get into and is very difficult to break out of. We get used to looking for things that could happen to us or the ones that we love. Worry for other people renders us powerless because we cannot control their actions and the situations that other people put themselves in. The worry habit has become so much a part of some peoples' lives that it would take a great deal of discipline to break it. There is also a perception that worrying about our children or loved ones is a way of expressing love for them. This could not be further from the truth.

Fear plays a large part in many of the steps to feeling good so I will cover it in more detail further on.

Anger is a very effective block to our feeling good. It will often show itself as either aggression or depression. Both of these are very destructive to us. Aggression is anger projected out and it is aimed at other people or property. It may come out as road rage, domestic violence, brawling or hooliganism. Depression is a more common manifestation of anger, it is anger turned inward against the self. It will often instigate very self-destructive actions and inner dialogue. When we are depressed, it is hard to associate the feeling with anger as it is deeply buried. Most of us will have experienced some level of depression at some point in our lives. This will often be circumstantial. It may be a death, lost job, money problems or a divorce or split. Anger occurs when something happens that we don't want or we feel powerless to influence.

Fear will usually be about a situation where anger will almost always be projected onto a person, whether or not they are actually responsible for what happened. Anger comes from the child aspect of ourselves. It is often expressed in a very childish way.

The source of our anger is usually in childhood. This then forms a trigger that brings the anger to the surface every time we find ourselves in a similar situation. For instance, if we were rejected by a parent in childhood, every time we experience rejection in relationships, work or friendships, we will feel the anger just as we did before.

One of the reasons why anger and depression is such a problem in the world is because we are so afraid of the negative power and force of our anger so we do everything we can to keep it at bay. This means that we fail to process it safely and move on from the person or situation that created it. We then carry the anger around as part of our baggage.

Guilt is another emotion that we carry around with us that severely obstructs our ability to feel good. Not only do we feel bad from the guilt itself but also the belief of our guilt will have a knock on effect on our self-worth, self-esteem and sense of deserving. When we perceive ourselves to be guilty, we must therefore be punished. We will then either punish ourselves or we will allow others or life to do it for us based on the choices we make.

Guilt is a completely subjective emotion. We choose to feel it and believe ourselves to be guilty. I have noticed that people who do dreadful things and cause untold pain and havoc in other people's lives rarely feel any guilt whatsoever. In contrast, those who are sensitive, kind and caring and spend their lives fulfilling the needs of others, will feel huge amounts of guilt when it is not warranted. We can see from this that the feeling is not real or rational and serves no useful purpose to society.

One of the problems with guilt is that it has no external or physical expression, unlike fear, anger and sadness. Consequently the guilt can become quite corrosive and may end up attacking the body. There are certain areas of life where guilt is most prevalent. These are parenting, relationships and in the family particularly with elderly relatives. We often feel guilt when we believe we are responsible for other people's happiness. When our actions fail to make these people happy or even make them unhappy, we may feel guilt. We have to take on the belief that we cannot be responsible for the happiness of others, only our own. To many this will sound selfish and this will be what the guilt will tell us. We are rarely thanked for the sacrifices that we make for others. It needs to be done as an unconditional expression of love or not at all.

It is essential that we off load the guilt we are carrying from the past and not let it devalue us or our lives. This will often involve reassessing and perceiving the things that we have done in the past differently. We need to see that mistakes are an invaluable part of our growth and learning. What does not work or make us feel good is there to show us that we need to adopt a different approach in future. We do not need to beat ourselves up for ever. As parents we need to accept that all parents do the best they can with the knowledge and resources available at the time. When we know better, we do better. This does not mean that we should feel guilty for what we did not know in the past.

We may well hurt people inadvertently along the way. This is often because these people have become dependant on us and believe that we should fulfil all their needs. This is not healthy and the kindest thing we can do is remove them from the dependency so that they have to learn to stand on their own two feet. We do not need to feel guilty for this, even if the person is hurt and angry as a result. We also need to learn not to choose to feel guilty in the future.

Sadness is another emotion that prevents many people from enjoying life to the full. It feels like they are carrying this heavy weight around with them and often they do not even know what the sadness is all about, it is just an ever-present energy. Most pain and sadness is due to loss and separation. This may create issues around abandonment and rejection. If we do not process our feelings, we will end up carrying them around with us.

When we have been hurt in the past, we will often respond to this by withdrawing, shutting down and keeping people at arms length so that they can't hurt us. This form of protection is completely self-defeating. It will ultimately create the very thing that we are trying to avoid, namely hurt. When we shut people out, they get the message not to try and get close to us or they will be rejected. We will end up feeling isolated, lonely and as if no one likes us or wants to be with us. This then represents the very rejection and abandonment from which we are trying to escape.

We all have patterns from the past that we keep repeating time and again. We will be totally unconscious of many of these patterns. In some ways we are like robots on auto-pilot. Our past thoughts, words, actions and feelings are programmed into our unconscious selves and when we find ourselves in a position that we have been in before, we react in a way that makes us do, think, say and feel as we have done in the past.

We will have patterns in many areas of life like relationships, at work, with money, in the home and in friendships. Some of these will be positive and work well for us, while others can be very destructive. When a pattern is well established, the compulsion to repeat it is very strong. The first step to healing and removing a pattern is to be aware of it. We have to become more conscious and see what we create in our lives. If we don't like it or it doesn't make us feel good, we need to change it.

Our beliefs play a huge role in creating who we are and what happens to us. Whatever we believe about ourselves or about the world, we will manifest as our reality. We will either draw to us people or situations that reinforce our beliefs or we will choose to perceive things in the light of our beliefs. They will then appear to be that way even when this is an illusion. Our earliest experiences will have formed our beliefs. Sometimes parents, teachers or siblings will have told us what to believe about ourselves but this is often just a projection of their issues and bears no relation to us. Other times, we will create our own beliefs based on our interpretation of how people behave towards us. For instance, if our parents were always too busy to spend time with us, we may conclude that we are not loveable or worthy of their time. In reality this will be far from the truth but if we carry this belief, it will usually be reinforced.

We need to become aware of what negative beliefs we are carrying from the past that are playing such a large part in creating the life that we are currently experiencing. Common beliefs are things like: I am not good enough, I am not worthy, I am stupid, I'll never amount to anything or I am not loveable. These need to be removed and new positive beliefs programmed in.

Our baggage from the past will often relate to certain areas of life. The three biggest of these are relationships, childhood and death and bereavement. These areas all require us to process and move on from the four emotions that we have already looked at. Sadly, our culture does not feel comfortable with the expression of emotions and teaches us to repress them rather than process them and let them go.

Relationships will always create a great deal of emotional rubbish. This is partly due to how relationships are perceived by society and the expectations that are put on them that can never be realised. We have all been brought up on fairy tales and for many people there is a belief that our partner will rescue us from whatever circumstances we are in and will sweep us off our feet and make us happy forever after. This is a very tall order but in the early phase of a relationship this seems to be possible. However, this is not real and when reality sets in, so does the disillusion, hurt and anger. We even fool ourselves that the problem is not with our perception of a relationship but that this person is simply not "the one" and we have to keep on searching for this elusive person. Because many relationships go on way past their sell by date, a great deal of damage and baggage can be created in that time.

Most people do not unpack the baggage from past relationships before embarking on a new one. As a result all the old issues, anger, pain, guilt and fear are brought into the new relationship and will often get projected onto the new partner. I always think it is a mistake to go from one relationship to another without taking time to heal, process and learn the lessons that the past union provided. Without letting the rubbish from past relationships go, we increase the likelihood that our subsequent ones will not work out.

The things that we need to let go of most from old relationships will usually be anger, hurt and low self-esteem as well as patterns like control, jealousy, nagging, infidelity or dependency. Low self-esteem is particularly significant in this. We allow people, our partners and life to treat us to the level of our self-esteem. If it is very low, we will put up with abuse and appalling behaviour without complaint. We need to go into a new relationship already feeling good about ourselves rather than expecting the relationship to make us feel good. Control is another common relationship issue. We have to realise that it takes two people to create this pattern, one to control and the other to allow the control to take place.

When we have been hurt or rejected in a previous relationship, we will often try to protect ourselves by shutting down and not allowing anyone to get close to us. This will almost certainly doom any other relationship we get into and bring even greater unhappiness. The willingness to open ourselves and share that deep, vulnerable core of us is what defines a true relationship. Without it, we can only relate on a very superficial level.

Childhood will play a huge role in our ability to make us feel good. Many of us have had big issues to face in childhood. This could be things like abuse, divorce, death of a parent or sibling, poverty, illness or an absence of love or nurture. The more sensitive we are, the more intensely we will feel these things. As adults we will often try to compensate for what we did not have in childhood in an attempt to make us feel better. This rarely works. The child within our inner selves will still feel all the fear, pain, anger or powerlessness from the past. It then becomes as if we are two separate people; the sorted strong, confident adult and the damaged child. The adult works with the head and logic, while the child is very much the emotional, creative part of us. Some people deal with this situation by shutting down the emotions altogether and staying in the head and adult mode. Anything that may put them into emotions or child-state must be avoided at all costs. This is often the pattern of the workaholic. They do not even like having holidays because it would involve play and leisure. As I have stated before, if we disconnect from our emotions in order to avoid feeling bad, we block any possibility of feeling good.

Instead of compensating our adult selves, we need to heal and let go of the baggage of childhood. I know of no one who has got through childhood unscathed. Even children who were loved, nurtured and protected will have issues.

Clearing baggage from the past is probably the most important step to feeling good. However, it may not be something that we are able to do on our own. I have a firm belief that simply talking about something is not the same as letting it go. This is particularly true of emotions. These are a tangible energy that needs to be physically released from the body and not just the mind. Letting go of the past also involves making active changes in our current lives. If we carry on doing the same things, we will end up creating the same outcomes.

TIPS FOR LETTING THE PAST GO

1) Start to be aware of the impact that your past has on your life. This may involve some honest soul searching and letting go any denial. If you want to know what you are carrying from the past, you have only to look at what your life is like. Are you in a state of struggle and survival? Do you feel you are progressing and moving forward on your chosen path? Are you in healthy and loving relationships and friendships? Does your work give you what you need, both in terms of money and fulfilment? Do you have time for your interests, hobbies and personal growth? How do you feel most of the time? Ask these questions of yourself and begin to build up a picture.

2) Look at your emotions. Does fear stop you from doing things or keep your life small? Are you a worrier? If so, what sort of things do you worry about?

How do you cope with anger? Do you suffer from depression? Does your anger explode aggressively and cause pain or fear in those around you? Are you frightened of your anger and keep away from any possible conflict? Do you know what makes you angry and where it comes from in the past? Do you have any safe means of expressing your anger?

Do you feel guilt? Are you a people-pleaser, trying to do for others in order not to feel guilty? Can you say no to people without feeling guilty? Do you have parental guilt? How do you punish yourself for your guilt? Who makes you feel guilty?

Do you carry pain and sadness inside? Have you had any bereavement that you did not sufficiently process? Do you cut yourself off in order to avoid being hurt? How else do you try and protect yourself? Was there any separation or abandonment in your past? Do you feel comfortable expressing your pain? Do you feel weighed down by your sadness? What makes you cry? (If you need more help and information about these emotions, I would recommend that you read my books on releasing fear, anger, hurt and guilt.)

3) Look at your patterns. There will be different patterns in the various areas of life: relationships, work, money, home, family and friends. Scrutinise all of these. Ask a friend or relative what they think your patterns are. They may see them more clearly than you can. Do not get defensive! When you have isolated a pattern, look at the effect it has on your life. Is it positive or negative? Look for the start of this pattern. Go back to that initial situation and choose to perceive it differently. Then make a conscious effort to think, feel, and act differently when you find yourself in a situation where the pattern plays out. Remember, it will take several times to reinforce a new pattern, doing it once or twice is not enough. Look at how you want to feel and what you want to create in forming your new patterns.

4) Look at the beliefs you have about yourself and life in general. Notice how many of these appear to be true in your life. If you do not know what you believe, look at what you attract to you or what seems normal in your existence. See what the sources of these beliefs are. Did your parents feed them to you? Are these beliefs part of your culture, society or peer group?

Is there any religious influence that have given you your beliefs? Did you come to these conclusions yourself or by how people have treated you or behaved around you?

Decide what beliefs work for you and create positive outcomes and what ones don't. Choose to let the negative beliefs go, understand where they have come from. You might want to do a process to remove the beliefs from your unconscious mind. I would suggest writing on a piece of paper three times: I RELEASE THE BELIEF……….. I REMOVE IT FROM MY CONSCIOUS AND UNCONSCIOUS BELIEF SYSTEMS. Then burn it as a symbol of release.

5) Have you had any relationships in the past which had any baggage attached to them? Did you feel hurt, rejected, angry or guilty? Were there any major issues like abuse, control, infidelity or betrayal associated with any of these relationships? What was the legacy that you took on from these relationships? Do you find it hard to trust people? Are you cynical and unwilling to let anyone get close to you? Have you become the controller in order not to be hurt again?

See all of these things as if they were packed in suitcases with big labels like ANGER stuck on them. Do a process where you visualise yourself throwing these bags onto a bonfire. Breathe each emotion or issue <u>out</u> from your physical body. If there is unfinished business from any relationships, you may need to write a letter that you will burn and not send. In this letter you want to say all the things you were unable to. Express your anger and hurt onto the page. No one will read this, so you can say what you want as graphically as you need to. Burn it as soon as you have written it. Do not keep it. You may want to make your peace with a previous partner. This may involve forgiving them or yourself for what occurred. Make sure you do not project any feelings or issues onto a current or future partner. Learn the lessons of what works and what doesn't in relationships and take this knowledge into any subsequent partnerships.

6) What were the overriding issues from childhood? What are you carrying from that time? Do you have low self-esteem? Was there abuse of any sort? Were there any separations, either of your parents from each other or with

you? This could be things like divorce, illness, death or boarding school. Did you have problems with siblings? Were you bullied at school or at home? Did you feel loved as a child? Did you get your needs met consistently? Was there poverty or struggle in the home?

Look at how you may have compensated for issues in childhood as an adult or with your own children. It is the child inside that needs the healing and attention and unless this happens, the baggage from childhood will negatively impact on your life. Visualise the child in you throwing out the bags labelled with the issues and emotions that you are carrying. Put them in the bonfire and see yourself nurturing that child.

7) Have you lost a person that you are close to? Did you fully process all the different aspects of grief like shock, anger, guilt and pain? Did you keep busy or do things to avoid feeling these emotions, like drink or take drugs, prescription or otherwise? Did you have to close off areas of your life in order not to feel? Sometimes these unexpressed emotions will result in a breakdown years later.

Allow yourself to feel your emotions. Breathe them out of the body. Throw the baggage from bereavement into the bonfire.

KEY THREE
STAY IN THE PRESENT

*"When we yield to discouragement,
it is usually because we give
too much thought to the past
and to the future."*

STAY IN THE PRESENT

We work in a linear, space-time continuum and consequently there is only this moment that is real. The past is past and the future is an unknown quantity that we are yet to discover. Having said this, the vast majority of us miss the present because we are putting our focus of attention somewhere else. We lose the opportunity to use this moment to create the wonderful future that is available to us and also to fully enjoy the benefits that being in the present brings.

The main reason that we tend to miss being in the moment is because we are not conscious or awake enough to notice or enjoy it. If our focus of attention is on anything other than the here and now then we will miss it. Most of us are like robots, going through our day. We are programmed for the day, particularly if we are in a routine. We will get up, get dressed, have breakfast, go to work or take the children to school. The chances are that each one of these things is done in the same way each day. We might not even remember anything about them because we are on automatic pilot. Sadly, many people spend their whole days on auto-pilot.

The fact is that the more we can remember and recall about our lives, the more awake, conscious and present we are. I often see clients who can't remember anything about their childhood and very little after that. This is because they were not present at the time. This does not mean that they weren't there because, of course, they were but they were not *in* the present, they were somewhere else. This could be in their minds, in a book or television, daydreaming or even in a higher meditative state. People often use meditation as a means of escaping the present. We also see a pattern that occurs when there is a trauma or a very difficult time like bereavement. We almost leave our bodies in order to get away from the pain or the shock. People will often say later that they cannot remember anything about that time because they were not really there. I see many people who have been sexually abused and it is very common to lose all memory of the incidents. This is because they remove themselves in order to escape the trauma.

The fact is that the more unconscious we are, the less power and control we have to influence the course of our lives. We are very passive and let life or other people make the decisions as to what we do or what happens to us. This is a very dangerous state of affairs and this alone should be enough incentive to want to be in the present.

One thing that prevents us from living in the present is the habit of projecting our focus of attention into the future. One of the most common ways of doing this is with worry and fear. For many people worry is a way of life. They spend most of their time thinking of all the negative things that *could* happen to them or their loved ones. When we worry, we feel as if the thing we are worrying about has already happened and we are powerless to do anything because there is nothing we can do about something that does not exist. I would say that about 80% of what we worry about never happens. The 20% that does occur, we cope with and will often find that we grow and learn from the experience and come out stronger, more confident people. For instance, if we are worrying about an exam or job interview, this is something that we know is going to happen in the future. What we worry about is the outcome of the exam or interview. What if I fail? What if I am rejected? What if I am not good enough? What if I make a fool of myself? Most tests and challenges stretch us and give us a better understanding of how to function optimally.

Fears and phobias have a huge impact on our ability to live in the moment. We are always looking ahead of ourselves for where any possible dangers lurk. They make us limit ourselves to a huge degree. The things we are afraid of rarely happen but we can end up attracting them to us by the degree of fear we have.

One of the best ways to overcome fear is to learn to live in the moment. As I have said my definition of fear is that it is a projection into the future about something that has already happened in the past. You will notice from this that the past and future are featured in this definition but there is no mention of the present. The fact is that if we are in the present, there is no room for fear. Even when we are in the middle of a crisis, we are so busy dealing with it, we do not need to feel fear. I was attacked once and noticed that while I was in danger I was so intent on what I needed to do to survive that I was very calm. It was only when the attacker was gone that the fear arrived. When we are in the moment, we can acknowledge that in this moment I am safe. I have shelter, food, clothes, warmth and everything I need to get on. I often recommend that people who are prone to panic attacks or anxiety just put their focus outside of themselves on what is *now*. There is no fear.

There is another way that we project our focus of attention into the future. That is through fantasy and daydreams. This may seem like a harmless exercise and it will often strengthen our imagination. However, this is a form of escapism. We want to take ourselves away from the reality of our lives and create in our minds the life we would like to have. The problem is that this fantasy stays in our minds and takes us further away from making our dreams come true in reality. Where fear is a negative projection into the future, fantasies and daydreams are a positive projection and may make us feel good temporarily. In the same way that what we fear does not happen, nor does what we fantasise about. Fantasising can become an addiction like many other external feel good substances. However, when we compare our real lives with the fantasies, we come down to earth with a bump. We then want to escape again and so the addiction goes on.

Many people only survive and get through life because of their dependency on fantasies and would be most unwilling to give them up. I am not for one moment suggesting that we give up our hopes and dreams; far from it. What I am saying is that it would be more productive to invest the energy we use to fantasise in doing the things that would bring about the real thing, instead of an illusion.

I have noticed that fantasy addicts are filled with fear and do not actually want to risk failing or have the responsibility that making their dreams come true brings. Also, we are in complete control of the fantasy; in reality we do not have the same ability to control other people or the things that life throws at us.

Another way in which we put our focus of attention into the future is through our expectations. Most of us have expectations about people and situations. Once again, our expectations always anticipate something that is going to manifest in the future. Expectations are the road to disappointment. Inevitably, most things in life will be different from how we expect them to be. Sometimes they will be better. Most of the time our expectations are too high and so we set ourselves up to feel bad and be disappointed. I am sure most of us can identify with going to a party or a social situation where we set our expectations too high and we felt let down and deflated when it did not live up to them. Equally, when we are not looking forward to something, it often comes up trumps and we have a great time. The trick in life is to have no expectations but to decide to get the most out of whatever is on offer. Expectations look for a specific outcome and if this is not forthcoming, we write off the whole experience and miss the real gift that was available to us.

In our lives there is a natural flow that we need to be in tune with. There is a time and place for everything. Many people try to pre-empt what lies ahead on their path and will often create confusion and struggle. We may be aware that a change ahead is inevitable but we can only make that change when we get to it. For instance, we may be in a relationship or job that is no longer satisfying. We know that at some point we are going to be moving on. If we jump the gun on making the decision, the next thing in our lives may not be fully formed or ready. This puts us in a state of limbo, confusion and even chaos. We can only make clear decisions when our options are given to us. The analogy I use for this is if we are going along a road and we know that there is a junction ahead where we are going to have to change direction. We will only know which way to go when we get to the junction and can see the signpost that will clearly point to our destination. If we get ahead of ourselves and veer off the road trying to anticipate the direction, we will get lost. When we stay in the moment, we will know the right time to make changes or the big decisions in life. These will be clear and the transition will be easy and painless. On the other hand, we will create struggle and fear if we put ourselves ahead of the game.

Timing is so important if we are to make the most of life. Particularly in things like relationships, timing is crucial. I believe that each relationship has its own shelf-life. This may be a lifetime or a matter of weeks. When we break a partnership before it has reached its natural end, we will often be left in limbo, with a painful wound to tend to. We will have unfinished business with our partner and often feel powerless to move on. We sometimes think that we are going to save ourselves a lot of pain down the line by cutting the relationship short but the reverse is true.

A more common scenario is to let a relationship go on way past its sell by date, it will usually descend into acrimony and become very destructive. In an ideal world, if the parting took place at the right time. there would be no negativity attached to it.

Stress is another sign that we are not living in the moment. When we feel stressed, there will be many things that we have to do or a deadline to meet. We focus so much of our attention on what we have to do in the future to fulfil our obligations or make our deadlines that we waste a great deal of time worrying about what we have to do, instead of getting on with doing it. It is imperative that we deal with these situations by putting our full attention on the job in hand and when we have finished that we go onto the next one. This way we are more efficient and do not allow the sense of overwhelm and helplessness that often comes with stress.

Many people wait for their lives to happen and to come to them. It could be argued that they are in the moment. If we are completely passive in the moment and put out no energy or effort to create the things we want in our future then nothing will happen. It is not about waiting for our lives to come to us, it is about sowing the seeds and putting into action the things that we would like to have in the future.

It is not just projections into the future that keep us from living in and enjoying the moment. Many people seem to live in the past, in a time when they were happy or had success or triumphs. This is another form of escapism and is not healthy. When we live in the past, we will often hold on to the physical things that represent or remind us of the past. Often our lives are totally cluttered up with things from the past and we are unable to move on. It might feel quite comforting to live in the past but if we are looking backwards, we cannot see where we are going and this keeps us stuck.

The reason it is so essential to stay in the moment if we are to enjoy life and feel good is because what we think, say, feel and do in this moment will decide what we manifest and feel in the future. If we want good things to happen, we have to plant and nurture the seeds now. Every second is an act of creation. In a nutshell, if we put out negative energy, we will get negative things back. If we put out positive energy, we will create good things and if we put nothing out, we will get nothing back.

We need to acknowledge that for every action there is a consequence, this is one of the Universal laws. Most of the time we do not marry up the consequences with the actions that created them. We rarely take responsibility for what the reality of our lives are. We are not helpless individuals, victims to the whims of what God, fate or life throws at us. We are powerful beyond measure and have in some way or other played a part in everything that has happened to us or not happened for that matter. The secret is to learn and become aware of what we do that does not serve us and bring in more of what does. We can only create the future that we want if we are fully awake and in this moment and sowing the seeds for what our ideal or optimal life is.

We have seen in this chapter that the main reason why people do not live in the moment is because they do not like what they see there. Escaping from it into their heads, the future, the past or by watching television or into fiction or films is not the answer. If we change nothing in our lives, nothing is going to be any different in the future. It is significant that this is the third step to feeling good because we are not going to want to be in our present life, if we do not clear out the dross and deadwood and if we are not prepared to let the past go.

Not being in the moment is a habit that we need to learn to break. In the early stages this will take dedication and discipline. First, we need to be aware of what our patterns are in this area. What do we do rather than be fully engaged in our lives at this moment? We may well be so detached from our lives that we are not even aware of this. We can observe ourselves and see what we do think and feel. We can see if we are always onto the next thing or whether we take time to enjoy the moment. What circumstances put us in the past or the future. On an average day how much time do we spend living in the moment and do we ever consciously plant seeds that will create a pleasant and enjoyable future? In order to break a habit, we have to be aware of what it is and what the trigger points are.

The most common way that we avoid living in the moment is to go into our heads and get caught up in all our thoughts. Most of us will have had the experience when driving that we go so deep into thought that miles of the journey go by without our having seen anything or been aware of how we have driven. In effect we lost that time totally. Consequently, one of the methods that we can use to bring ourselves into the moment is to take the focus of attention away from the mind and put it on external things. Look at and notice what is going on externally. It might be looking out at nature and watching the birds or squirrels or noticing things about the people around us. This is the first step, to be awake and aware and in the moment. If we are not conscious, we are in danger of missing the signposts and opportunities as they are presented to us.

From this point we can begin to see how we want to feel in this moment. We can also see if there are any blocks to our feeling the way we want. If there are, we need to put into action the effective removal of these blocks. Happiness is a decision and we can only decide to be happy in this moment as that is all that exists. Once we are engaged in the moment, we can begin to plant the seeds for our future. Some of these will bloom and others may not. As long as we have no expectations and are not attached to any specific outcome as this may only lead to disappointment.

Another advantage of being in the moment is that we are open to receiving inspiration, guidance and intuition, this needs to be acted on at the first possible opportunity or the moment may be missed. I see so many people who waste so much inspiration by not putting it into any action or falling into the trap of fantasising the outcome instead of creating it.

TIPS FOR BEING IN THE PRESENT

1) Look at the degree to which you are in the moment. On an average day what percentage of your time is engaged in the present? A helpful way to

do this is to clock how much you remember or noticed about what you did or what happened yesterday. Are you aware of your thoughts and thought processes or do they just waft through without your being aware of them? Start to make changes by listening to your thoughts and begin to direct them into areas that will be profitable for you. Notice what *is* around you and be awake and aware of other people and the opportunities that are around.

2) Notice how much of your life is on auto pilot. Do you follow the same routines every day? Be aware that if you do something that is very repetitive, you will switch off and do it automatically. Start to break the routine. Take a different route to work or school, when washing or cleaning or doing things round the home, make it fun and different. If you have too much structure around you, begin to deconstruct it. Notice how predictable you are and spring some surprises on your nearest and dearest.

3) Are you prone to fear and worry? This means that you are projecting negative scenarios into your future. Not only does this make you feel bad in the moment but it is programming a negative future for you. Catch the thoughts that put your fear and worry into action. As soon as you are aware of them, STOP. Bring yourself back to the moment, look at what is going on, what song is on the radio, what the weather is like or what is going on outside your window. Then repeat a positive affirmation like I AM SAFE AND PROTECTED AT ALL TIMES. Keep repeating this until the fear or worry subsides. Do not indulge in the "what if....." scenarios.

4) Do you have expectations that you put onto people and situations? Are these expectations high? Have you noticed how often in the past you have felt let down or disappointed? Make a conscious decision not to have any expectations and be willing to accept and see the gifts in anything that happens. ACCEPTANCE IS THE KEY TO HAPPINESS.

5) Do you daydream and fantasise about the things that you want to happen in your life? What are you escaping from that is in your life now? Do you make any positive steps to making your dreams a reality? Are you afraid of failing so you won't put yourself to the test? Be aware that you run the risk of life passing you by with nothing of any significance

happening. Start to look at realistic outcomes that are within your power to create and in every moment plant or nurture the seeds that could create that outcome. It might help to look at the desired outcome and then break down all the steps needed to achieve this. In the moment just focus on the next step and what needs to be done.

6) Do you make decisions or initiate change before you have reached the crossroads in your life? Are you in a state of struggle? Do you feel confused and unclear as to your options? Are you lost on your path? Have things taken you off your path in the past? If so, it may be necessary to track back to where you deviated from the clear path rather than remaining lost and unable to find your way. Alternatively, do you refuse to take opportunities when they present themselves preferring to stay on old familiar territory? What are you afraid of?

7) Do you live in the past? What specific time of your life are you drawn back to? Was this a time of success and happiness or one of struggle and failure? What was going on and how did it make you feel? How is your life now in comparison to that time? Do you hang onto memorabilia from the past? Could you let this go?

8) Begin to notice what you think, say, feel and do. Do not censor them to start with, just observe. Start to marry up these thoughts, words, feelings and actions with the consequences of your life. Start simply. Notice if you feel good or bad and then track back and see what created it. For instance, if your mood suddenly drops, look at what has just happened? Did you have a fear thought? Did you go back to a difficult time in your past? Did you tell yourself off for something? Equally, if something made you feel good, track back to what it was. Be aware of what things make you feel bad or good and then consciously let go the former and bring in the latter.

9) Start to sow positive seeds in the moment. Make sure this correlates to what you want to manifest in your life. For instance, if you want to be a famous author in the future, in this moment you need to be writing or researching the book that will enable you to become that author. Each moment is an act of creation.

10) Stay grounded and realistic. This will keep you in touch with what can and cannot be achieved. Try to stop any 'pie in the sky' schemes.

11) Choose to be happy in each moment. Even when you are doing routine or everyday tasks. This can be enhanced by things that make you feel good, like your favourite music or being with friends who make you laugh or support you.

12) Go with the flow. Do not try and control it or try to predict or pre-empt where it will take you. Only make major decisions in life when you reach the crossroads and the options are clearly marked.

13) Notice and appreciate your surroundings. This will keep you in the moment in a positive way.

KEY FOUR
MAKE GOOD INVESTMENTS

"Money is only a tool. It will take you wherever you wish, but it will not replace you as the driver."

MAKE GOOD INVESTMENTS

Everything that we have, are and feel are the direct result of the investments that we make. We are the authors of our lives and our destiny is in our own control. Unfortunately, most people are totally unaware of this fact and continue to make very bad investments in their lives and suffer the consequences of doing so.

When I speak of investments, I do not simply mean in terms of money. This is not a guide to making a killing on the stock market. It is the investment of energy and what we put it into that I am referring to here. Money is certainly part of this and it is probably the most tangible form of energy that we work with. It may be easier to see our patterns of investment in terms of money and then apply these patterns to other areas of life. Money is simply an energy in the form of notes or coins that are used in exchange for goods and services.

The forms of energy that we invest in our lives as well as money are things like time, effort, attention and power. In every moment we are investing something. Often we are not conscious of where we are directing our energy and the consequences of it.

My father was a businessman and he studied economics. He never forgot his professor's definition of economics given to him at the start of the course. "Economics is the study of allocating a limited number of resources to an unlimited number of demands." Obviously, this is mainly referring to money. I would like to expand this definition to the whole of our lives. There are only twenty four hours in a day and we have only the amount of money that we earn or have and there is a limit to the amount of energy or effort that we can put into anything. Equally, there are endless things that we could do, make or have by investing this energy. We therefore have to make choices as to what we invest in and consequently create for ourselves.

Whether we have made good or bad investments is decided by what we get back or the return on it. If we get back more money, energy, fulfilment, satisfaction or growth than we put in, this will constitute a good investment and we can keep on investing in it until it no longer brings the same return. On the other hand, if we are making a bad investment, we will feel tired, drained, short of money, unsatisfied or unfulfilled. Sometimes this may be a close call to make as we get a mixed return on our investments. For instance, we might do a job that we hate, that leaves us exhausted, stressed and drained every day. However, we might get paid huge amounts of money to do this job. We have to weigh up whether the cost to our personal lives is worth it or whether the money and security are more important. This can be a difficult choice and many people struggle with this dilemma. I have to say that for many people in a situation such as this, their body will revolt and create disease like heart problems or strokes that force them to reassess their investments.

We need to take an overview of our lives and look in general at whether we are making good investments. Then we need to break it down and look at the specifics of what we invest in and whether we get a good return or not. If we look at our lives right now, do we have plenty of energy and enthusiasm for our lives at the end of the day? Is there more than enough money to provide for all our needs, wants and desires? Do we feel fulfilled and satisfied with what we do? Is our home and environment as we would want it to be? Do we feel loved, appreciated and valued by the people we have in our lives? If we can say yes to all these criteria, then we are making excellent investments and need to keep up the good work. We might find that we can answer yes to some of these elements and no to others. If this is the case, we need to reassess the balance of our investments. Alternatively, in general do we feel tired, apathetic, drained, unmotivated and unfulfilled. Do we escape into television, DVDs, the computer, drink or food? Are we in debt or feel that we don't have enough money to do what we would like? Does it feel like people use, abuse or take us for granted? Do we drag ourselves through every day, feel like there is no progression and that life is to be endured and got through? If this is closer to our reality, there is a serious need to change our investment pattern. If we don't, there is no way that we are going to feel good in our lives. Remember, if we change nothing, nothing will be any different.

I will now look at the various areas of life that we commonly invest in and see what some of the patterns may be. First, I will look at the workplace. We spend a third of our lives at work so this constitutes a vast investment of time and energy. We would hope that we would get a sufficient amount of energy back for such a large investment. However, money alone will never be enough of a return. Job satisfaction is essential. If we do not have satisfaction and enjoyment in our working life, this will be a sign that we are doing the wrong job. We might be in the wrong career altogether or it may simply be that we are doing it at the wrong place or in the wrong way. We need to decide which of these options is true for us and do something about it as soon as possible. I have a friend who did many jobs where he just put the time in and longed for weekends and holidays to get away. He has now found work that is creative, productive and he believes in what the organisation is trying to achieve. He loves work and cannot wait to get there. His bosses praise and appreciate him constantly and at the end of the day he has plenty of energy available to socialise or pursue his interests and hobbies. He has been in this job for years now and the positives have not lessened over time.

When we are self-employed or have our own business, it is even more important to make sure that we make good investments of our time, money and energy; our success and income depend upon it. We need to make sure that we are getting the best possible use out of our talents and strengths. For instance, if our strong points are our creativity or ideas, we do not want to tie up all our time and energy on administration or accounting. We would be much better served to delegate or hire someone to do these things.

If we are making bad investments at work all the symptoms will be there. If only a few are evident then this is a sign that a bit of tweaking needs to be done. We may need to change our hours, get some more help or support, renegotiate impossible deadlines or take sufficient breaks. However, if we are displaying many symptoms, this is a clear indication that we need to rethink our whole work situation.

Fear features strongly in our bad work investments. So many people spend a lifetime doing a job they hate because they are too scared to move on in case they fail or cannot earn enough to maintain their lifestyle. Many companies actually instil fear into their work force in order to control them. Rumours of cutbacks or redundancies will often make people work extra hours without more pay. Some people believe that their only chance of promotion comes with giving everything to the job at the expense of the rest of their lives.

Relationships are another area where we need to be aware of our investment patterns. Ultimately, the reason why relationships fail is due to either under or over investments. I always see it that there are two people and then there is a separate entity that is the relationship they have. Both parties need to invest in and work on the relationship in order for it to thrive. The elements that go into the relationship are love, respect, time, communication, support, money and fulfilment of needs. A common scenario that I come across is where one partner is putting about 90% of the investment into the relationship with the expectation that their other half will do the same. However, they will often only put the 10% needed to complete the partnership. Sometimes, the more we do, the less others need to do. I always suggest in these cases that the over-investor pulls back their energy to balance and mirror the amount put in by their partner. One of two things will happen here. Either the partner will increase their investment to take up the shortfall, in which case we were not allowing space for them to put their energy in. We can then increase our input until we are in balance. The other option is that we are being used and when we pull back, there is no increase of energy put in by our partner. This is a clear sign to get out of this relationship before we waste any further time or energy.

Many men believe that if they are bringing in the money that goes on the house, the bills and food, then this is all they need to invest in the relationship and it is up to the woman to do and give everything else. However, this does not constitute a balance of investments. One of the biggest and most contentious issues in a relationship is the man not pulling his weight around the home. In this day and age most women work and many bring in more money than their partners and yet are still doing the lion's share of work in the house.

When we are getting less out of a relationship than we put in, this will create a huge amount of resentment. Resentment can be very toxic and corrosive. It bubbles away under the surface and will often kill any love that was present before.

It may be necessary to negotiate our investments in relationships. This is particularly necessary when circumstances change like when children come along. Failure to do this will almost certainly result in a breakdown of the partnership and create a great deal of pain in the process.

When we feel good in a relationship, this is a sign that we are getting a good return on our investment. Ideally, if we are investing the right things in the partnership, we should both get more out of it than we put in and it will sustain and energise us.

In life there are going to be long and short term investments. In a short term investment we would expect to see an almost instant return. A long term one may involve a huge input of time, money and energy before we get anything back. New businesses and children definitely come into this category as any parent would agree. Ideally, there comes a time when our children pay back this investment and look after us and our needs in old age. Sadly, not all children pay back the energy but with any luck they pass the investment down to their own children and so the cycle goes on.

While it is inevitable that we will have to put vast amounts of time, energy and money into our children, it is essential that we keep this in balance and that we have other investments that are paying dividends to take up the shortfall. Many parents make the mistake of putting everything into their children at the expense of their relationship, their own interests and hobbies, their friendships and most of all at the expense of themselves. This is a recipe for disaster and will result in years of struggle, exhaustion and feeling stuck.

If we are parents, we need to look at how much we put into our children. Do we do everything for them and not make them take responsibility for themselves. Are we stressed, irritable, exhausted or on an everlasting treadmill? Do we have any energy left at the end of the day for anything or anyone else? Do we try and get some energy back through food or de-stress with alcohol? Do we live vicariously through our children? Do we dread the time when our children leave home? If these factors are a common part of our lives, it is time to rethink our parenting and how much the children take out of us.

Notice what our patterns in friendships are. Are we always giving more than they are? Are we the ones to phone or make arrangements to get together? Do we feel supported or able to call for help when we need it? We may behave differently in our various friendships. It is so important that we only invest in friendships that give back as much as we give. Some people are professional users and will cultivate those who might be useful to them. We know who these people are because we do not feel good spending time in their company. They may put us down or actually be quite jealous of what we have and are, they are rarely interested in anything that is going on in our lives. Any friends who use us, drain us or make us feel bad about ourselves need to be removed from our lives or demoted to mere acquaintances.

Many of us have a pattern of people-pleasing. We are incapable of saying no to any request for help or things. We feel guilty if we have to refuse anyone anything. There is often very low self-worth behind this pattern. People pleasers are constantly making bad investments because they are taken advantage of. Often they spend so much time giving to those who do not matter in their lives that they have nothing left to give to their nearest and dearest who end up suffering. This also creates a great deal of anger and resentment within that is either not expressed or taken out on someone close to us.

Guilt will often cause us to make poor investments. People manipulate us into doing what they want by using guilt as the weapon. Children and old people are very adept at this and we fall into the trap of playing the game.

Our home and environment is another area that most of us invest a great deal in. We spend a lot of time and effort cleaning and tidying our space and it is essential to our feeling good. It is hard to feel good in a dirty, untidy, cluttered place. Also, our outer home is going to be a good mirror and indication of what we feel inside. There are also things like DIY and gardening that we need to invest in to keep our homes at their best. If we do not enjoy these things and find it a huge chore, we would do better to pay someone else to and invest money rather than our time and effort to get the job done.

We also need to look at where and on what we invest our money. Obviously, there are the essentials like a mortgage, rent, bills and food. Where does the remainder of our disposable income get invested? Do we buy things that we don't need or use? Does it go on socialising or going out? Does it go on cigarettes, drugs or alcohol? Is there debt? Does money get put aside as savings or does all our money get spent? I would suggest looking at all the purchases we make in a week and observe what comes back from each investment? How do they make us feel? Remember there may be a short term buzz followed by guilt or feeling bad because it has added to our debt. These opposing elements need to be weighed up. For each purchase we can ask ourselves to what degree it enhances our lives. Notice the bad purchasing habits that have crept in. Before buying anything, check whether this thing is needed or will improve life in some way. If the answer is no, then let it go.

It is important that our investments are in our own power and control. We would not give all our money to other people to spend and choose for us. We are the best judge of what we spend. So often we let others dictate what we do and have and this is a recipe for disaster. Make sure there is no one in your life that is effectively making your choices and decisions.

Another way in which we make bad investments is in giving our power away. This is our inner, divine power and strength as opposed to our outer material or status power. Our inner power is our generator that churns out the energy that we have to spend. If we give away parts of the generator, not only do we deplete ourselves but we lessen the amount of energy output that we can generate in future. If we are constantly giving away our power, we are rendered completely powerless and are unable to function other than in a totally passive way. The good news is that we can take our power back. Most people try to get their power back by getting into a power struggle. This is a huge wasted investment of energy as we get stuck in battle with the person we gave our power to. We will give our power to people like our parents, siblings, bosses and anyone who tries to control or bully us. We also give our power away in relationships in the mistaken belief that our partner will give us a return on this investment by loving us and meeting all our needs. A power struggle will ensue and becomes a natural part of relationships. We will know when we have given our power away because we feel bad and helpless. The golden rule is that we only invest the interest or what we produce from our generator, we do not give away the capital or the generator itself.

We also invest in our beliefs. Whatever we believe, we then create as our reality whether it is actually true or not. We manifest what we believe in because we put our energy into these things. Sadly, most of the beliefs that we end up creating are not positive ones. We need to be aware of what beliefs we are investing in. To find this out, it may simply be a case of looking at what we have in our lives. We will have to see what we have already invested in and made happen. If we do not like what we have in our lives, we will have to look at making different investments.

When we look at our overall investments of time, money and energy, we need to get a cohesive strategy together. All the things and people that drain our resources need to either be removed from our lives or we need to drastically rethink what and how much we put into them. It is also essential to spread our positive investments over a variety of people and activities. This way, if one begins to go bad, the others can sustain the shortfall. However, if we spread our investments too thin, we cannot always do them justice and we may create stress in the process. It may be necessary to prioritise and keep some things on a back burner until we can put the right time and effort into them.

If we want to feel good all the time then it is essential that all our investments are working for us and not against us. This may involve some work and effort in the early stages but once the systems are in place, they will become self-generating and perpetuating and we can keep reaping the rewards. Every so often we may need to take stock and reassess various investments. Life is always in a state of flux and change and we can outgrow some aspects of our lives. If we are content to go with the flow of our lives, we will not get stuck in the past.

TIPS FOR MAKING GOOD INVESTMENTS

1) It is essential to be aware of where and in what you invest your time, money and effort. Make three lists: one for time, one for money and one for effort or energy. You are then going to take an average week and under each heading put the per cent that you give to each of the following areas of life: work, family, home and environment, relationships, hobbies and interests, socialising and personal self.

2) Next to each of these you are going to put the degree to which you do or do not get back the investment you put into all these things. This can also be done as a percentage. Anything less than 100% means that you are getting less back than you put in. For instance, you may spend 60% of your time at work but you may only get back in terms of money and satisfaction 50% of that input. This represents a very bad investment. Remember you assess the return on any investment on many factors: money, fulfilment, joy, love, enthusiasm, productivity, satisfaction, growth and learning. You will know if you are getting these things back because you will feel good and energised. Signs that you are not getting a return on your input are tiredness, exhaustion, stress, debt, apathy and lack of productivity and satisfaction.

3) If you are getting 80% or less back on what you put in you need to rethink what you are doing. You could get away with 80-100% as long as you are getting more back in other areas to balance out the shortfall.

4) Look at the degree to which you are in deficit and tackle the areas that are draining your resources the most. It is essential that you do this or you are in danger of becoming energetically bankrupt.

5) Once you have a clear picture of what you are doing currently, you can start to make positive investments. This may mean spending time with fun friends, taking up a hobby that you enjoy, saying no to people, asking for help or support, allowing your children and spouse to do more and take responsibility for themselves, pampering yourself, changing your job, demanding a raise; the possibilities are endless.

6) Take your power and control back from anyone that you have given it to. Make sure your inner generator is working to full capacity.

7) Keep tweaking your investments until you are in credit. Gradually increasing the return you get and then reinvesting it in other areas. If you experience a dip in your energy or money input, look at what has changed and reassess what you are doing in your life. Waste no time in clearing out the deadwood.

KEY FIVE
BROADEN YOUR HORIZONS

*"The person who risks nothing,
does nothing, has nothing and is nothing.
Only a person who risks is free."*

BROADEN YOUR HORIZONS

We all have what is known as our comfort zones. These are the area within which we function without being challenged. Our comfort zones will vary enormously from person to person and they work on many different levels. In an ideal world we would be constantly growing and learning and this growth will show itself in the expansion of our comfort zones. Anything within our comfort zones is easy and well inside our capabilities. Anything outside is an unknown quantity and will feel challenging.

The thing that will delineate the outer boundary of our comfort zones is fear. We know when we reach the edge of our zone because we experience nerves, anxiety or fear. Human nature will always try to get us away from any fearful situation, so we will tend to pull back when we find ourselves facing fear. Most of us will have tested and be aware of where our outer limits are and then content ourselves to live within those confines.

What we achieve and how big or small our lives are will correlate with the size of our comfort zones. Sadly, for many people this is very small indeed. Those who suffer from an excess of fear or things like panic attacks will often only feel comfortable in a few rooms in their home. They rarely go out and only then if someone else is with them.

We have different types of comfort zones and all of these need to be addressed and pushed back. The most obvious is the physical comfort zone and this works on two levels. For many people there is a physical area that they are familiar with and they are not happy going out of that area. They fear that they will not know where they are going and will get lost. The nerves kick in and usually stop them from venturing further afield. This pattern is stronger with women than it is with men and will often create a dependency in that we become reliant on someone else to take us where we want to go. Many women refuse to drive on the motorway and will take hours longer on a journey than is necessary or alternatively they may not bother to go anywhere at all.

The other type of physical comfort zone involves the things that we do. We may have a fear of heights and be unable to climb a ladder or go up in a lift. Many people will not fly or go through tunnels or go into water. The thing that limits us here is fear of being physically hurt or dying. This fear can seriously restrict our lives and limit what we do and where we go. There are some people who go to the opposite extreme and become adrenaline junkies. They are forever looking to push back the comfort zones by doing things like bungee jumping or rock climbing or abseiling. However, someone who has very large or non-existent physical comfort zones may not score so well in the other areas.

We also have a mental comfort zone. This will more often be shown to us in the work place. We all have an awareness of our capabilities and this will usually be what we have done before that is tried and tested. The boundary of our mental zone will be shown to us when we move into an area where we have no expertise. Fear of failure will usually be the thing that delineates our mental comfort zone. We may balk at doing a course or exams or avoid going for a promotion if it involves public speaking or leadership. I see so many people stuck in the same boring unfulfilling jobs because they are too scared to break out.

Our mental comfort zones are not purely in terms of our work. They may also restrict us in our interests and hobbies. We may love to sing or dance but are afraid to perform in public because we fear that we are not good enough. We may even want to do some charity or voluntary work but think we haven't got the skills to do it. The fact is that we only gain the skills and expertise by actually doing the things and learning on the job. Talking in public is the biggest phobia that people have. However, when we do it a few times and the world has not opened up and swallowed us, we find we have the confidence to do more and more and to bigger groups of people.

If we want to know the degree by which we are restricted by our mental boundaries, we have only to look at the progress we have made in our lives. If we have had a steady progression with regular promotions, if we have learned new skills, if we are constantly challenging ourselves to move on and grow, we are effectively pushing back our boundaries. However, if the reverse is true and we constantly shy away from learning new things or going into new areas, it is essential that we conquer the fear and start to broaden our horizons.

The third area where we may encounter restrictions is in the emotions. This will affect us in our friendships, relationships and in our social life. Here the fear is of being hurt emotionally. Many men in particular will fall down in this area even though they may do well in the other two. A great proportion of men and some women are in a state of what I call emotional shutdown. They may have been hurt in the past and then shut off from the emotions by staying in the head and avoiding people and situations that might put them back in touch with the emotions. This makes the emotional comfort zone very tight indeed. Our willingness to be open and let people into our inner selves and to see our vulnerability, shows that we are pushing back that boundary. Many people's marriages are conducted on a superficial, material, and physical level. Some people are horrified at the thought of opening up and letting their partner get close emotionally. Obviously, in a relationship the emotional boundaries are different from ones we would have with friends or social contacts but the principle is the same: we share a personal part of ourselves.

Many people have social phobias. They may be chronically shy and not know what to say to people. There might be a fear of being judged not good enough or boring. They may always be comparing themselves unfavourably with others. Whatever the fear and issues, it is important that we learn our social skills and practice them constantly and push back the social barriers. At the end of the day, until people get to know us better, they will judge us by our own estimation of ourselves. What we put out, we get back. If we are open and friendly, people will be open and friendly to us. If we make them feel good about themselves, that goodwill will come back to us. Ideally, we need to teach our children how to socialise and feel confident in social situations. These skills need to be learned and honed over many years.

We need to observe where our comfort zones are in social situations, in friendships and in relationships. How open are we? Do we pull back and hold ourselves back? How easy is it to say what we feel and be honest about our inner most thoughts? Have we shut down emotionally and made sure that no one gets close to us? There are huge rewards to be gained by pushing back our emotional limitations but it might require our letting go of some baggage from the past before we are willing to do this.

We have seen that fear is the thing that puts the restriction and limitations on our lives. I have noticed that where there is a great deal of fear, we will either be very victim-like or very controlling. Control is an immensely destructive pattern. We believe that in order to be safe, we have to be in control of our environment, the people in our lives and the circumstances that happen to us. Naturally, this is impossible. The only thing we *can* control is ourselves and our response to people and situations. Control freaks will usually have to make their lives very small in order to give them the illusion of being in control. It may extend as far as a spouse or family and home if enough fear or guilt are used but beyond that they cannot control and they know it. They will often have to isolate their partners from friends or family who they cannot control. Within the family they will use the 'divide and conquer' principle. They keep siblings at odds with each other so they cannot rise up together and revolt against the control. Ultimately, a control freak will always lose because eventually people will have had enough and leave. We must make sure that this need for control and the insecurity behind it do not play a part in our lives and very effectively keep us and our world very small. By giving up the need for control we can go with the flow and make our lives as big as they are meant to be.

When asked what quality we would like to have more of, the answer is often confidence. I define confidence as an absence of fear. To me, it is that indefinable quality that some term the 'x factor'. We can't put it into words but we all know it when we see it. It is an aura or presence that is there and we are usually drawn to that person. They will stand out in the crowd and somehow seem larger than life. Many of us want this confidence so much that we go to great lengths to try and get it externally. I call this a superiority complex masking an inferiority complex. We will try to get it through success, money or status. We also have to sell ourselves and tell everyone how wonderful we are. This will come over as being egotistical and is actually covering up a huge degree of fear and inadequacy. True confidence just is, we don't need to shout it from the rooftops, we just live it and be it. When we overcome and conquer fear, the confidence is a natural by-product. This absence of fear will mean that there are no limits to who we are and what we do and achieve in this world and we are then able to effectively fulfil our potential and mission on earth.

The process of broadening our horizons and expanding our comfort zones involves facing the fear and not letting it stop us. We know when we reach the edge of the zone because fears, doubts, worries or anxiety will surface. Instead of backing away and returning to the comfort zone, we can welcome these feelings, knowing that we have a chance to overcome them. Feel the fear and do it anyway, as the saying goes. We need to keep pushing out on all three levels: the physical, mental and emotional.

When faced with fear, we need to remind ourselves that it is an illusion, it only exists in our perception. We then need to bring ourselves back into the present moment and look at the practical steps we need to take to push through the fear and do the thing that is challenging us. By breaking these things down into bite size chunks and putting them into our present moment, the spectre of fear disappears. For instance, if we are bored and unfulfilled in our job but are afraid to move on, we can start to make moves toward changing the job by buying a publication with job vacancies, phoning an employment agent, ringing a local college to see if they offer new skills training, going to the boss to see if there are new opportunities within the present company, getting a new CV, telling friends to keep an eye out for new work and so on. All these things in themselves are not threatening but may be a stepping stone to a new life. Always do the preparation work. If you do nothing, you get nothing.

We only grow and learn through challenge. This is what pushes back our comfort zones and allows us to experience life at a much higher level. As I have already stated in this book 80% of what we worry about does not happen and the 20% that does constitutes the challenges that we need to grow and evolve. When we persist in staying small and comfortable in our lives, these challenges will come in ways that we would not choose for ourselves. They might be an illness like cancer, redundancy, divorce or a split or some kind of accident. These are what I call 'cosmic kicks up the bum.' They force us to change our patterns, to look at ourselves and to move on from situations. However, in the process we may end up going through pain, trauma, hardship or difficulties. At the end of this time we may well be back on track, stronger, healthier and forced out of unworkable situations. We can avoid the necessity of needing to have a 'cosmic kick up the bum' by setting and facing our own challenges. This involves constantly facing the fear and pushing through it, but it can be done in a healthy and controlled way. We can even learn to enjoy these challenges and find ways and skills to enhance the process. We need to constantly be looking out for challenges and opportunities that will stretch us and make us not rest on our laurels. One of the best ways to raise our feel-good levels is to face and conquer the fears and challenges that are presented.

Broadening our horizons is going to involve a degree of risk. We are going into unchartered territory for us and we do not know what we will encounter along the way. If we don't risk, we will never find out. Probably the two things that we fear the most in this process and that we are therefore risking are failure and rejection. It is imperative that we change our perceptions of these things in order that they do not block us in future.

Failure and mistakes are invaluable tools that we can use to help us grow and expand our horizons. They are simply there to show us what does not work. There should not be any emotional baggage attached to this realisation. As soon as we know that something does not work, we let it go and try something else and keep on doing this until we find what does work. It is an essential part of the process. Sadly, many people who do something and fail become so afraid of failure that they do not try anything else and get stuck and unable to move forward. This must be avoided at all costs. Welcome failure and mistakes as the guidance they are and do not waste any more time trying to make something work, move on and try another route. Unfortunately, society is not very tolerant of failure and this perpetuates the fear.

Rejection is there to show us that something or someone is not right for us. This is not personal and it is not meant to hurt. Once again, it is there to steer us away from the wrong course and to help us find the right one. It is far better to be rejected for a job or relationship than to be in it if it is wrong for us and we have to extricate ourselves later at great personal cost. When we can see the gift in even the most difficult of circumstances, we set ourselves free to face the challenges.

We do need to take risks when pushing out our comfort zones but I must make the distinction here between risk and recklessness. This is not about trying to achieve the impossible or setting ourselves challenges that we do not have the tools or expertise to fulfil. So often we start out with a no win situation and we would be wasting our time, energy and money trying to make it work. It might be a risk and a challenge to jump off a cliff without a rope but the chances are we would end up dead or maimed as a result.

This is not just about setting up challenge for challenge's sake. We want to invest our time and energy going in the direction that will best support our life purposes and the path we are meant to be on. To do this we have to enlist the support of our intuition. This invaluable part of us will show us the opportunities and challenges as they present themselves in the moment. This way we do not allow fear to build up and stop us. If we are not in the moment, the chance will pass us by. We need to listen to the intuition even when fear raises its ugly head. Remember, the fear is only there to show us that we have reached our outer limits and that we have a chance to push those limitations further away. Welcome it! We can also use the intuition to find the easiest and most painless way of overcoming the challenge. It can save a huge amount of wasted energy and investment in the process.

When facing the fear in doing our challenges, we can change our perception of it. Excitement and fear bring up the same feelings in the body. They are the opposite sides of the same coin. We can choose what label we want to put on it. Fear will paralyse us but excitement will encourage us to do the thing that is pending. Both feelings are projections into the future but one is negative and the other positive. One makes us feel good, the other bad. We can choose to feel excited about the new territory we are going to explore.

I did a fire walk once and it taught me a huge amount about pushing back the fear barriers. I was asked if I wanted to do it on the same day that I had written a paragraph in a book about facing our fears and pushing back the comfort zones. Because of this synchronicity I knew I was being tested and as I am not very brave, I wanted to say no but I felt I had to say yes and rise to the challenge. There was a period of three months before the walk was to take place and every time I thought about it I could feel my stomach lurch in fear. My way of dealing with this was to tell myself that if it was genuinely dangerous, it would not be allowed to take place and then put it out of my mind and come back into the moment. On the week leading up to the walk I developed a mantra that I said every time the fear came up, "I trust the process." Clearly we would be shown how to walk through 1200 degree centigrade hot coals without burning ourselves. Interestingly, on the day of the walk my fear turned to excitement and I felt the urge to giggle constantly. The walk was amazing and the burning embers felt like walking through soft warm sand. I did it three times and the high and satisfaction was immense. Not only did I conquer the potential pain of the fire but I had a serious back problem that caused me great pain and it disappeared that night. The effect that I was left with was the sense that if I could overcome the fire which is in reality potentially dangerous, then I could certainly overcome my fears which are illusions and do not exist in any real form. I immediately wanted to look for new challenges to stretch me still further. It interested me to observe that the people who did not gain a huge amount from the experience were the ones who had put too high expectations on it! (See step three.)

The feel good factor comes when we have faced and overcome the challenge. In a nutshell, the good feeling is as a result of banishing fear. Fear is what makes us feel bad and removing it can only serve to make us feel good. We then want to perpetuate the higher state of energy by pushing back our limitations still further. If we took this process to its furthest conclusion, we could indeed conquer fear altogether and this would in effect ensure that we feel good ALL THE TIME.

TIPS FOR BROADENING YOUR HORIZONS

1) Look at where the boundaries of your physical, mental and emotional comfort zones are. Observe how limited and restricted your life is as a result.

2) Look back at your life and see if there has been progression. Do you have more courage and a wider experience of life or have you regressed and don't dare to do things and go places that you did in the past?

3) What are the fears that you encounter that keep you stuck in your small existence? For instance, fear of failure, fear of being hurt, (emotionally and physically) fear of not being good enough, fear of rejection and fear of being judged and criticised. Do you know where these fears come from in your past? Where have you experienced these things before?

4) When you encounter fear, notice if your pattern is to pull back. Begin to change this. Be determined to face the fear and push through it and do what you want.

5) Begin to set challenges for yourself that will stretch you and take you into new territory. If you don't like to leave your familiar area, start to gently go further afield. Go and visit someone in a new place or go to a town you have never been to before. If you have fears and phobias that limit you physically, begin to face them. Go on a ride in an amusement park or climb a ladder. Get support and help to do this. You could even work up to doing things like skydiving or bungee jumping if you really want to push back those boundaries. Set challenges in the mental and emotional areas. Learn some new skills or put yourself in situations that you would not normally go into.

6) Look at whether you have an issue with control either as the controller or as the victim of it. Either way this will dramatically limit your life. Let go the fear that is feeding this pattern and trust that you will be given what you need at the right time.

7) Use your intuition to know how and where to face and push back the fear blocks that are standing in your way on your path. Do not be reckless

and challenge fear for the sake of it. This would constitute a poor investment of your time and energy.

8) Use your desire to be truly confident as the motivation for facing and releasing fears. Change the perception of fear and see it as an opportunity and not a threat.

9) Change the label of fear to excitement. The feeling is the same but the result is different.

KEY SIX
BE CREATIVE

"When you find that you are not feeling joy, ask yourself 'when did I last sing? When did I last dance and when was I last enchanted by a story?'"

BE CREATIVE

I have chosen being creative as an important key to feeling good because I know for myself that some of my best times and biggest highs have been as a result of some aspect of creativity. There is nothing else in life that is capable of giving us such constant satisfaction.

Creativity is one of the things that raises us as humans above the rest of the animal world. It puts us on a higher evolutionary strata. We do not see creativity in any other species.

I have put this key in the middle of this book because the one prerequisite we need in order to be creative is that we are not stuck in survival. When we are in a survival mode, absolutely all our energy goes into just existing and getting through every day. Fear has featured very strongly in all the previous five steps and it is the fear that puts us in a struggle, survival mode. Once we have begun to master the fear and we have cleared the detritus from our inner and outer world and we are making investments that give us time and energy back and we are willing to change our patterns and go into new territory, we can start being creative.

Creativity covers a vast range of things. We can get bogged down in thinking that it just covers subjects like art and music and if we weren't good at these things at school then its not for us. In reality, every moment is an act of creation. What we think, feel and do goes into making our future. However, we can also invest in our creativity on a far bigger scale and make things happen in our lives.

It is also important to acknowledge that our creativity is not just something we indulge in at weekends or when we have the time. We can bring creativity into absolutely every area of our lives. This includes at work, in the home, looking after children, while driving the car or waiting at the bus stop. Even something mundane like writing up a report or doing the accounts can be creative. I am one of those people who gets very excited about finding an interesting font on the computer and I have to find the right one for what I am working on. I find this enormously creative.

The creative process in all its different stages is very satisfying and raises the feel-good quotient considerably. It starts with a thought, an idea or flash of inspiration. However, for many people this is as far as it goes. They fail to put the inspiration into action. This stage is crucial. It does help to put the idea down on paper as this begins to crystallise it and puts it in a more tangible form. Next we need to get the tools and products needed to make it real. We also have to allow for trial and error as part of the process and we may need to do a good deal of tweaking before we have a finished product that we are satisfied with. It is important to note that the bit in the middle where things go wrong or do not turn out as we imagined or where it looks like it is going to be a disaster, are essential to the process. Most projects will go through this stage. It is crucial that we don't get downhearted and stop at this juncture. We have to push through and come out the other end. Many people have a pattern of not finishing what they started and many potentially brilliant things never reach fruition. I think that we also have to acknowledge that the creative process is a long term one. Very few people will be good at what they do the first time. We have to learn from our mistakes and hone our skills over time and see a steady progression and improvement with every effort. I cringe at how primitive some of my past creative projects seem in comparison to what I produce now and no doubt I will look back on my present creations with equal criticism.

One of the reasons why being creative has such a feel-good factor is that we have a product to show for our efforts. We can see a tangible result from the energy we have invested. So much of what we give and do does not have the same feeling of productivity and this can be very de-motivating. I have a client who works very hard in a job that involves liaising between other groups in the company. She is now leaving the job because she is so frustrated at not seeing a tangible product or result from all her hard work. No doubt the product does come into being further down the line as a result of her efforts but she does not get to see it. It is so important for our job satisfaction that we have a physical thing to show for our work or a clear indication that we have made a difference in the world.

We all have creative energy within us and as with any energy this needs to flow and be channelled into aspects of our lives. If we are not using this energy it will get stuck and blocked and it will make us feel that way as well. Interestingly, our creative energy is very closely related to our sexual energy. This makes sense as sex is one of our best acts of creation. Just as with our libido, we have to use it or risk losing it.

When we do something creative, it is a very active process. There is a universal law of energy that says that we get back what we put out. This is how we get back a great deal of positive energy from what we create. Most of us spend a great deal of time doing very passive activities like watching television. We do not have to put much effort into it and this will limit the level of satisfaction that we get out of it. Many people only have the energy to flop in front of the television at the end of the day. Before television people would devote a large amount of time to creative pursuits and learning these arts would constitute a great deal of their education. One of the biggest excuses for not doing creative things is that we don't have time. However, I am sure if we worked out how many hours we spend watching television or doing some other passive activity, we would see the real picture. For myself, I often use the television as a background while I focus on doing creative projects. It is interesting to notice that the words creation and reaction are anagrams of each other. However, one is active and the other passive.

Creativity is our expression of ourselves. It will be totally individual and unique. It is a way of showing who and what we are. We can express our emotions through it and it is one of the most effective ways that we can show our innermost feelings and thoughts. We live in a very repressed world and anything that gives us a safe way of expressing ourselves has got to be positive. This is why we should not worry about how good or bad something we do is as long as it is a true representation of our thoughts and feelings.

There is also a very positive knock-on effect to our creativity, it can inspire and move others and raise their feel-good quotient. I know that most of the times that I have been moved to tears has been as a result of someone's creativity. It might be a piece of music, a work of literature or poetry, a beautiful painting or a performance. There have been countless times when I felt the hairs raise on the back of my neck and have goose bumps and the urge to cry when I have been touched by one of these things. It is as if something has reached in and touched my soul. Creativity has this amazing magical ability and we need to give this gift to others and inspire them to find the limits of who and what they can be.

I have always believed that we are all meant to have many strings to our bows in terms of what we do in life. In order for us to be whole and balanced, at least one of these strings needs to be creative. If we are doing the right thing for ourselves, it will constitute a good energy investment that will cover us in other areas of life that are not bringing us such a good return of energy. I belong to a drama group and I see people coming to rehearsal wilting and exhausted after a hard day's work. At the end of the evening their energy is restored and they are full of life and fun.

We also have to decide whether we want to make our creative interests our career. Many people fall down on this one because their strengths lie in creativity and yet they are having to make a successful business that can support their lifestyle from it. This pressure often puts too much strain on us and we are unable to enjoy our creativity as fear comes into the equation. This is why I believe it should be one of the things we do. If it brings in money that is great but we have other means of supporting ourselves as well. I have many friends who do many different things to bring in their incomes. One is often creative, one is therapeutic and one may be an ordinary mainstream job. This will often work very well and creates variety and interest in their lives.

We have to find the areas of creativity that suit us. This may involve some trial and error. What do we enjoy? What inspires us? What gives us a buzz when we do it? It is important to note that we do not have to be very good at it in order for it to be right for us. For instance, we do not need to be a budding Renoir in order to paint. We can use colour and shape in order to express what we want. The more we do, the better we will get. We can also express our creativity in more practical ways, it could be cooking, gardening or decorating. We might want to try some new skills and see how we get on. This may involve checking out some adult education classes and see what does it for us.

We can also look at this issue of creativity from another angle. What do we want to express in the world? What effect would we like to have on people and then work backwards to find what we can create that will achieve this? Do we want to inspire, entertain, educate or beautify? What gifts do we have that would lend themselves to these areas? We also need to acknowledge that we are all cogs in a great big machine and our output may play a crucial role in producing something that is bigger and more important than we can imagine.

Another bonus to our being creative is that it is a very effective means of keeping us in the moment. It can keep us from worrying or from harking back to the past. When we are doing something creative, our focus of attention is outward and not stuck in the mind. We have to concentrate on what we are doing and that is something that is in the present. When we do something creative, we are able to put our troubles aside and do something that is ultimately very productive and satisfying.

Within our creativity we must not get bogged down in any sense of failure or success or good or bad. This will seriously block us and make us look for the approval of others in what we do. The only criteria that matters is that we enjoy and feel good about what we do. Anything we get on top of that like money or praise is simply a bonus; it should not be our main motivation.

TIPS FOR BEING CREATIVE

1) Look at how much creativity plays a part in your life right now. Are you a creative person who does not have the opportunity to express it? Do you think you are not creative and therefore do not pursue any interests?
2) What do you enjoy doing? Are you a practical, technical type or do you like to use your flair and imagination?
3) Make a list of the creative things you enjoy. Make this as broad as possible and do not miss things out because you don't think you are very good at them.

4) What inspires you in terms of other people's creativity? Do you love reading or going to concerts or the theatre? Do you enjoy craft fairs or watching DIY or gardening programmes? These will be areas that you could look to develop your own abilities.

5) What effect would you like to have in the world? What possible ways could you find to make that happen?

6) What do you need to express from inside you? You may want to get emotions out in a positive way. This is also a way in which you can show people who you are. It is also a personal voyage of discovery: you can find out who you are.

7) Has your creativity been blocked in the past either by other people's comments or by your own criticism? Are you afraid of being not good enough or being judged for what you do? Let yourself know that you are doing this for yourself and do not look for praise or approval from those around you.

8) Start the creative process going in your life. Look for the idea or inspiration. Do not waste any time to take it to the next stage or you will lose the impetus. Make a plan of action. Get the materials or knowledge that you need to put this into action. Make some time and space for yourself. Do not have any expectations that you put on yourself. Know that you might not be as proficient as you would like to start with; you will learn. Use your mistakes and failures as an important part of the process. Make sure you finish what you start so that you do not get into a pattern of never finishing your projects. Get support to hone any skills that need developing. Be encouraging rather than critical of your output.

9) Have creativity as part of your everyday life and do the things that bring the greatest satisfaction and feel-good factor.

10) Rejoice in your productivity and channel it into where it can make a difference in the world.

KEY SEVEN
LIVE LIFE ON PURPOSE

"The purpose of my life is not just to survive but to thrive with passion, compassion, humour and style"

LIVE LIFE ON PURPOSE

One of the most frequent questions I get asked by clients is "What is my purpose?" If we are not living our purpose, there will be an enormous sense of emptiness or a void in our existence. When we find and perform our purposes, we feel whole and at one with everything. It would be virtually impossible to be completely fulfilling our purposes and not to feel good as a result.

I believe that each and everyone of us has a potential or optimal life that our higher selves mapped out for us before we came in. Within this life will be the challenges and lessons that we have opted to learn. There will also be our lifework and what we have come to do and change in the world. This is our purpose on earth. Sadly, very few people get to fulfil the purposes that they have. Many of those who have completely managed to live up to their potential will be known to us because they stand out from the crowd and will have made an impact and difference in the world.

When we are young and we have our goals and ambitions as to whom and what we want to be, we often see success and money as the summit of our existence. Many people are totally driven to achieve their objectives and remove themselves from their lowly beginnings. It is only once we have achieved these goals that we can begin to see how empty they are and they often bring as many negatives as positives. Once we find this out, we have to go along with the pretence. In our society, we tend to envy and look up to people based on what they have rather than who they are. The rich and famous become the focus of our attention and we believe they must be having a magical life as a result of their wealth and privilege. In many cases this could not be further from the truth. They have a vested interest in keeping up appearances and perpetuating the illusion. For many successful people, it is more important for things to look good to others to cancel out the disappointment of it not feeling better. We have only to see the huge divorce rate among the rich and famous to see that it is not all that it is cracked up to be. I am not saying for one moment that being rich is bad or wrong; on the contrary. I am just saying that it becomes empty and meaningless if it is not underpinned by our fulfilment of purpose.

Once again, it is nigh on impossible to be on purpose if we are in a state of struggle and survival. All our energy gets invested into just getting by and making it through each day. When we are in a state of struggle, we are often taking ourselves further away from where our purposes lie. I always liken struggle to going against the natural flow of our lives. In effect, it is like trying to go up a down escalator. We have to expend a huge amount of energy to make any progress and we usually end up in the same place as where we started. In contrast, the flow of our lives will navigate us to the mapped out, optimal life that we came in with. At the right points we will be presented with the challenges and opportunities that will provide us with the growth and means to fulfil our purposes.

Fear will once again be the biggest block to our finding and fulfilling our purposes. It is fear that will keep us in the survival state and prevent us from being aware that there is a whole other existence that is there for the taking. The vast majority of people in this world work on a survival level, eeking out an existence that does not have room or the luxury of being connected with a higher purpose.

Control is an element that keeps us stuck in struggle and prevents fulfilment of purpose. It is virtually impossible to go with the flow and to be in control, they cancel each other out. When we have the need for control, we will be working with a great deal of fear and this will effectively block our connection with our higher selves or soul. It is within this connection that we are able to be guided to our purposes and how they may be made manifest.

There are always some general aspects to our purpose that we are all here to do and then there are the individual means by which we fulfil the group purpose. The purpose of the soul is to evolve. This is done by the learning and growth that we achieve. In essence our evolution is created by our raising our energy to higher and higher vibrations. With each increase, we feel better, we understand more, we function better in the world and we increase the group consciousness. If we raise our vibration, we help to lift even the most stuck individuals at the lower end of the scale.

Ultimately, if enough people raise their energy high enough, it will lift the whole of humanity out of the fear/struggle/survival mode. This is what we are here to do, to play our parts in this whole amazing process.

The purpose of the soul is to evolve. On a human level this translates into our objective, which is to conquer fear and create Heaven on Earth. It is only fear that blocks this evolution. Personally, I do not believe in hell as a place or a punishment. The only hell there is exists here on Earth and it is not a place, it is a state of being that is created out of our believing and investing in the illusion that is fear. In any given moment, we will be allying ourselves with either fear or love. One will create hell on Earth and the other Heaven. The choice is ours. It is hard to grasp how we could have created a world that is so entrenched in fear when in reality fear is not real and is only created in our perception of life and living. Fear will feel real and will often act as a magnet to the things that we are afraid of. This then seems to confirm that our fear was real and so the cycle goes on.

Built into our purpose is an understanding that it will make a difference in the world. Some aspect of what we do and are needs to contribute to raising that energy vibration on this planet. Many people get stuck in seeing their purposes in terms of selfless giving and doing for other people. If we are not giving and doing for ourselves first, we will have very little to give and will go into burnout mode. Whether our purposes involve inspiring, healing, teaching or entertaining, we have to learn to give these things to ourselves. This also means that we are going to be wise, healthy and happy while we are doing our purposes.

Money and abundance are often huge blocks to our finding and doing our purposes. In actual fact, if we are doing our true purpose, abundance is built into the equation. The only way this is not true for us is if we block it from coming. There is a warped belief that sacrifice and suffering are good and make us more worthy or noble people. This could not be further from the truth. Sacrifice and suffering add to the negative energy in the world rather than raising the positive, which is always going to be the main element in all our purposes. If it does not feel good, it is not the right thing. Many of us also have a block about charging for our time, energy and expertise. This is crazy because for the world to work, we have to have a balanced exchange of energy. This goes back to our making good investments and that step must be kept in mind as we establish what we do and how we work in the world.

There is a process that we can go through to discover what our individual purposes are. First, we look at what gifts, talents and abilities we have. These can be very broad and seemingly unconnected. We come into life with all the tools that we need to do what we have come to do. What those tools are will be a clue as to what we might do with them. We may have to break away from society's stereotypes as to what talents are. Are we creative? Are we good with people and children? Do we have good organisational skills? Are we good communicators? Are we good at linking people with the goods and services that they need to progress? Are we good problem solvers? Are we very intuitive? Do we have a good eye for colour and design? Are we good at making people laugh? The list is endless. It does not help to be modest in this process. If we find it hard to know where our abilities lie, it might help to ask our close friends and family. They will often have a clearer picture of us than we have.

Once we have an idea of where our strengths lie, we can go to the next stage. We can decide what we enjoy or what we would like to be good at. This is key because our lifework should always be enjoyable. We can also look at whether we have the personality type that is out there on the front line or whether we enable others to shine and work to their potential levels. Each role is of equal importance in the grand scheme of things. Remember, some of our skills and abilities may be dormant and it is only when we awaken them that we discover how good we are or how easy it is to raise them to a higher level. Life is going to be a progression. As long as we are learning and moving forwards, it doesn't matter how skilled we are when we start off.

When we have a good sense of ourselves and our gifts, talents and abilities, we can then turn our attention to the outer world. What do we feel strongly about? What would we want to change if we had the power to do so. What would we want to be remembered for when we are gone? It is fine to be very idealistic in this part of the process, we can get realistic later on. Here, we can see if our concerns for the world involves adults, children, animals or the environment. What would we like to stamp out in the world, like poverty, war, abuse, disease, cruelty, persecution or pollution.

Within this process we have to be aware of the ripple effect. We are the stone that drops in the pond. We can inspire, teach, entertain, facilitate, heal, care for others and impact people beyond our awareness. However, we have to go about this in the right way in order to maximise the ripple effect. So many people see the big issue or problem and try to fix that and waste vast amounts of time, energy and money in the process. We have to start by *being* the change that we want to make in the world. I had a client who was passionately involved in creating peace in Iraq following the first gulf war. She set up a committee of eminent professionals in many different fields to try and make a difference in that troubled country but she just encountered blocks and struggle in the process. I very much admired her dedication and commitment but during the course of her session I began to realise how troubled she was within herself and her home life resembled a war zone with a destructive daughter and difficult relationship. Even her committee were constantly at odds with each other, wanting to get credit and praise and be top dog. I realised that this woman could not possibly create what she wanted in the world if she could not achieve it in the areas where she did have influence. If she wants peace in the world, she has to find peace within herself first and foremost. She then has to create harmony in her home environment, she can then bring that quality into her working life and let it filter through to all the people she connects with. If the ripple effect is in full flow, there will ultimately be changes made at the furthest reaches of our pond but we may never be aware of what they are and the part that we played in creating them. Our job is to set the process in motion.

The changes we want to make in the world start with us. If we want to remove poverty in the world, we do not give all our money away, this simply adds to the problem. We learn abundance awareness and pass it on to others. If we want to abolish the abuse and cruelty to children and animals, we have to look at how we treat ourselves first. Do we say horrible things to ourselves? Do we allow people and life to treat us badly? Do we make choices that create negative outcomes? We cannot influence others if we do not do it for ourselves. Once we have worked on ourselves then we have the tools and wisdom to give to others to enable them to follow our example. We often make the mistake of trying to help those who seem the most desperate and needy. In reality, we will make the most difference by influencing and inspiring those who are not so different from us. I always use the analogy of the pyramid. Wherever we are in terms of our evolvement will determine how high up the pyramid we are. We will see the people at the bottom of the pyramid as being the most needy of our help and salvation so we focus our attention there. We waste huge amounts of energy trying to make a difference here but these people are stuck in survival. They only care about getting through each day. Our greatest area of influence will be those who are on the step below us. They are ready and able to progress to our step. In turn, we would look to those on the step above us to provide what we need to grow and evolve to that level. When the process is in action, the ripple effect will be in place. The people at the base of the pyramid will elevate out of the depths due to the help and influence of those who have already learned how to get out of the mire. We can only teach what we have already learned and put into practice.

Some peoples' purposes may be very flashy and high profile, while others might feel that they are making very little contribution. It is important not to think this way. Being a good parent is probably the hardest job in the world and the legacy of this will pass down the generations and make a difference to countless people. This is a good example of the ripple effect in action. What we give to our children can pass to their friends, work mates and their own children. Much of what we do may not be seen on a physical level; it may be energetic and therefore hard to quantify. The film 'Its a Wonderful Life' depicts this very well. A man who lives a simple, small town life thinks he is a failure and tries to commit suicide. He is shown by an angel how different the world would have been if he had never been born. He had no idea that the little things he had done positively impacted on the whole community. We will never know the extent to which we have influenced the positive energy in the world but as long as we are doing our best and actively raising our own vibrations, we cannot fail to pass it on.

While we must not judge ourselves if our purposes are not as obvious or as striking as others may be, we must also ensure that we do not keep ourselves and our purposes smaller than they are meant to be. Remember, the full extent of our lifework or mission will be part of our potential lives. There are many reasons why we would want to seem smaller than we are. It is part of human nature to want to blend in with the crowd and not stand out and dare to be different. The belief is that if we put our heads above the parapet, we will get them shot off. Unfortunately, life reinforces this belief and pattern. It is the children who are different and do not fit into the norm who will tend to be the ones bullied at school. This is sometimes enough to shut them down and their unique, special gifts never see the light of day. We make ourselves small to make others feel comfortable with their smallness. We go down to the lowest common denominator rather than being part of raising everyone to the highest level.

We are often afraid of our potential and power as it may seem like too much responsibility and we may fail. The higher you go, the harder you fall, as the saying goes. This fear is once again an illusion. If we are on our purpose, we cannot fall back and we are only responsible for ourselves. We do not have to carry all of humanity, we have only to show the way to those who want to follow.

Our greatest asset in our desire to find and fulfil our purposes on earth will always be our intuition. This will give us all the signposts we need to take us along our mapped out path. We will only ever be given the next step along the way. This is a process that unfolds as we go along and it is important that we do not miss out any of the vital stages that allows us to learn what we need to know in order to fulfil our purposes. When we listen and act upon our intuition, we cannot fail to reach the potential we came with.

Many people are aware of the gifts and abilities they are meant to be using in creating their lifework but never actually put them to work. These may become part of the fantasy or something that they will do at a future date. We may use the excuse of waiting until we retire or the children leave home or when the house is sorted out. There is not a moment to waste! There is only now and we are meant to be working towards our mission and lifework at all times. We may be learning lessons or honing our skills.

I believe the things that challenge us in childhood are part of the training we need in order to do our lifework. Who better to understand an issue than someone who has experienced it and found a way forward from it? This might also be a clue as to what area we are meant to be working in. For instance, if we were subjected to abuse, alcoholism, death and bereavement or poverty, then these might be areas in which we are able to help others. When we have this understanding, it makes sense of what we have gone through and puts a positive slant on the situation.

Just as with our creativity, it is important that we see that we may need to do a variety of things in order to completely fulfil our purposes. These things may seem very diverse but they will make use of all our various talents and abilities. Some of these things may constitute our paid work and others may not. We can do our lifework even while earning a living doing something else. As long as we do not find ourselves deprived, anything goes.

If we want to know the degree to which we are already reaching our potential and purpose, we have only to look at the levels of satisfaction and fulfilment that we have with the things that we do. In life we are never static, whatever level we are at now is meant to continue to increase. If it doesn't, then this is a sign that we have deviated from our mapped out path and we need to find our way back to it.

I have called this step 'Live Life *on Purpose*' because there are two aspects to the phrase "on purpose." Firstly, we want to fulfil our mission but we also want to put intention behind our actions. We do it on purpose as opposed to by accident or passively. Intention is immensely powerful and will make what we want happen. We need to affirm that we have the intention of fulfilling what we have come here to do, namely our purposes.

TIPS FOR LIVING LIFE ON PURPOSE

1) Are you aware of what your purpose is? On a scale of 1-10 to what degree do you think you are on course for fulfilling it? Have you viewed your objectives in terms of success or material gain?

2) Make sure that you are not stuck in fear, struggle or survival. If you are, then your first objective is to elevate yourself above this by letting go of the fear and turning to your inner guidance as to how to get off this treadmill.

3) Do you try to control your life and environment instead of flowing with it? If so, resolve to let go the control and begin to flow with and not against your life and path.

4) Acknowledge that you are here to play your part in raising the energy vibration in the world. Look at the part you are playing in this NOW. Are you adding to the positivity or negativity in the world? Look at where you are negative and begin to make changes.

5) If you do not know what your purpose is, start to do the following process. Make a list of what you are good at.

6) Make a list of the things that you enjoy or would like to be good at.

7) What would be the changes you would most like to see or make in the world?

8) Apply these changes back to yourself. To what degree have you managed to achieve these things within yourself and the areas that you influence around you?

9) Be aware of the ripple effect and know that you are the pebble. What you put into your life will filter out from there. Note whether it is a negative or positive. BE the change that you want to make in the world.

10) How would you like to leave your mark and be remembered? This could be in a big or small way.

11) Make sure you do not impede your progress by trying to stay small and invisible.

12) Whatever you are meant to be doing, do it NOW. Don't put it off to sometime in the future.

13) Listen to your intuition. Allow it to let you know what you are meant to do and how to best achieve it.

14) Make sure you live your life ON PURPOSE. Put intention into what you do and are.

KEY EIGHT
HARMONISE YOUR ENVIRONMENT

The only measure of success that counts is the degree of inner peace, harmony and happiness that we achieve.

HARMONISE YOUR ENVIRONMENT

This key to feeling good does incorporate a couple of the other steps. We cannot harmonise our environment if we have not cleared our clutter first. No matter what else we do, it will not have much impact on us if the clutter is still there. The harmonising process is also a very creative one and it is a good area into which to channel our creative energy.

We have to keep in mind that this is going to be very individualistic and we must not be influenced by other people or fashionable trends of the day. In essence, what we are doing is to make sure that everything we have around us resonates with our own personal energy. Given that our whole purpose is to keep raising that energy vibration, we can see that harmonising our environment is going to be an ongoing, ever-changing process. Most of us cringe now if we look back at what we wore or the things we chose to bring into our homes twenty or thirty years ago. Yet at the time, we thought they were the bees knees. No doubt they totally reflected our personalities and energy levels at the time. It is important that we let go of clothes, furniture and things that do not reflect us now. We do not want to get stuck in the past or prevent ourselves from evolving.

Colour is one of the most important ways in which we can start to harmonise. Colour is simply another form of energy and we will be in harmony with some colours and not others. It has been found that colour has a huge influence on us and our moods and feelings. Colour has even been used to heal various ailments that we have. It has been found in prisons that certain colours will calm the inmates while others will make them more aggressive. The calm colours will be things like blues, greens and mauve. The more active colours will be red, orange or yellow. When deciding what colours to paint various areas, it is imperative to keep this in mind. Red might help stimulate passion in the bedroom but it may also stop us from sleeping. The calmer colours are much better suited to bedroom areas. Equally, we do not want to be too relaxed in areas where we work or socialise, so colours that stimulate work better here. There are also vast energy differences in the various shades of the same colour and we have to find the exact shade that works for us.

I find that a lot of people are quite scared of colour. Their clothes will often be black or very drab and in their home environment they will opt for white, cream or very neutral shades. There is often a fear of being seen or expressing themselves in case they are judged or criticised.

When we are choosing what to wear each day, we need to tune in and be very spontaneous. If we are aware, we will know exactly what colour we need to get us through the jobs of the day. We may not realise how important it is to get this right and what a difference it can make. Red will give us confidence and energy. Purple can help connect us to a higher level of awareness. Blue will be calming and help with our ability to communicate. Pink will help us to get in touch with our more feminine side. Black, when not mixed with another colour can appear sinister, severe or as if we have something to hide. White has a feel of innocence and purity but if it is not mixed with another shade may feel very barren. We need to make sure that we make a conscious decision what to wear. Even if we have to wear a uniform or have a strict work dress code, we can give ourselves the colour boost in our underwear.

Harmonising with our clothes is a daily, ongoing process. It is important that what we wear helps to make us feel good, it raises our confidence and self-esteem enormously. It is also important that the style and fit of our clothes is right. There is nothing worse than feeling uncomfortable or self-conscious. Our clothes also need to be an expression of who we are. Going along with all the latest trends without reference to our own personal style can result in a loss of identity.

Once we are satisfied that our clothes express and harmonise with who we are, we can turn our attention to the next layer which is our home environment. We will always have rooms that we feel more comfortable in than others. Even these can be improved on. First, we can look at the colour of the walls. Does it resonate with us and is the paint work in good condition? If the answer is no to either of these, then it is time to get out the paintbrush.

For each room that we have, we want to maximise the energy flow and make sure that we feel good and well disposed to the activities that are meant to take place in that room. Very small changes can make a huge difference to the energy of a room and consequently how we feel when we are in it. Feng Shui, or the Chinese art of placement has been very popular in recent years. It is governed by a set of rules as to where to put things and ways of minimising any negative aspects in our homes that may impact on our lives. I have been in houses that have received the full treatment and there were so many corrective bits and pieces that it actually detracted from the energy of the room. Since we are the ones who have to live in a place, it has to harmonise with us and there are no rules that apply to everyone.

Placement of furniture and things will be a very important aspect of harmonising our environment. We just have to use the trial and error method here and keep tweaking until it *feels* right. Do the furniture first. Make sure everything in the room is needed and used or enhances the feel of the room in some way. If not, take the extraneous things out. There is a very fine balance between having too much or too little in a room, both in terms of furniture and things. When we hit this middle ground, the energy and feel of the room will be at its optimal level. When placing things, symmetry and balance will play a part in making it feel good. We also need to make sure that all the ornaments and pictures in the room resonate with us in terms of their subject matter. We may have been given them or bought them during a different phase in our lives. We can also look out for pictures that lift our mood.

When we have sorted out the colour scheme and the placement of furniture and things, we need to bring in the other things that will further lift the room energy. For me, cut flowers are essential. They are not a luxury, they are a necessity. I immediately feel the change in the feel of the room when I put fresh flowers in. If they are scented then this is even better.

Plants are an absolute must in our homes. This is for a variety of reasons. There is the obvious benefit in that they look good and bring nature into our environment. I believe that we do not realise or give credit to the full extent of what plants do for us. First, they take the carbon dioxide that we breathe out and turn it into life giving oxygen that is essential for our existence on earth. It has also been found that plants absorb toxic substances and remove them from our environment. These may be chemicals or toxins that we use as part of our everyday life. It is essential to have plants in places like our kitchens where there may be a higher concentration of these substances. I also believe that there is another subtle but important role that plants play. They take on and absorb our negative emotions and pump out positive ones. Plants are the great transmuters on every level and play a vital role in our lives.

When choosing plants, they need to resonate with us. We also need to find the right places to put them. Here size does matter! We don't want a plant to dominate a room, nor do we want it so small that it has no impact or use for us. Once again, trial and error is the best way to find what works well. The healthier a plant is the more it will raise the energy levels in a room.

In harmonising our environment, we have to take into account all our senses. So far, we have concentrated on sight and feel. Our sense of smell is often the most neglected of the senses and compared to other animals is very dull. We can introduce things like essential oils into our homes. Each oil has different properties and it is a question of using ones that we need. Some are relaxing, some stimulating, some have a purifying effect and others are very healing. If we have a burner in our living and sleeping areas, we can use the oils needed for the activities that we do in those rooms.

Sound is another area that can play a huge part in harmonising or disharmonising our lives. A beautiful piece of music can lift our spirits to extraordinary heights. I belong to a resonance choir which uses sound to connect with and heal parts of the mind, body and soul. It is very powerful and after a session I feel a sense of oneness and of being in harmony with myself.

We also have to be careful what disharmonious sounds we let into our environment. Anyone with teenagers will know what it is like to have awful music played loudly in the home. Some of the modern songs work on a very low or negative vibration and this will infiltrate into the energy of the house.

It is one thing harmonising our homes but we need to extend this into the workplace. We may actually spend more time at work than we do at home. Depending on what we do, our ability to influence the energy of the workplace may be limited. Many people work in an environment where there is no fresh air or natural light. There is something called "sick building syndrome." Here, the people who work in the building will be prone to higher rates of sickness and depression than the norm. They may find that they are tired all the time and find it hard to concentrate and be productive. The obvious solution to this is to get out of the job but if this is not practical then other things must be put in place to minimise the damage. Plants are going to be the first things to set in place for all the reasons that I have already given. They will at least absorb some of the negativity. In a recent survey it was found that the productivity of people who put a plant on their desk increased about twenty per cent. It would also be a good idea to get out of the building at every opportunity, use lunch breaks to take in as much fresh air and natural light as possible. If you can have flowers to lift the mood, this will help. Bring colour and inspiration into the space in whatever form you can. See if you can influence any other workers or bosses to make positive changes to the environment. If you do have autonomy in your workspace, bring in all the elements you would in your living space. Make work a place that you want to spend your time.

So far, I have concentrated on harmonising things in our outer environment but there are other less tangible areas that are equally important to harmonise. First, we have to make sure that we are in harmony with our inner selves. So many of us are in a constant state of inner conflict. If this is the case, no matter what we do in our outer world, it will not impact on our inner state. Conflict is caused when different aspects of ourselves want, think and believe different things. The more opposing the things are, the greater the conflict. We waste vast amounts of energy on these conflicts and they usually end in stalemate anyway. For instance, one part of us may be ambitious and want to get on and succeed, while another part of us is scared and wants a small simple life. Both sides will debate their corner without any headway being made.

In my unique brand of therapy I work a great deal with what I call sub-personalities. It is these that create a great deal of the conflict. Common personalities that are often key in our inner conflicts are things like the tyrant, the rebel, the saboteur, the victim or the hermit. With my clients I disperse the negative energies of these personalities and use the strengths and positives to work with us and not against us.

There also may be conflict between our adult and child aspects. This will often be true if we have had a difficult or abusive childhood. These patterns may re-emerge within us with our adult selves taking on the role that our parents played in our childhood. By healing and letting go the past, we can change this dynamic and the conflict that goes with it.

The last area that we need to harmonise is with the people around us. Once again, there is very little point in having a wonderful home environment if we are always at odds with or rowing with the people that we have in it. Sometimes we have to accept that there are people who are on such a different wavelength from us that we cannot resonate with them. We then need to look at whether we have to have them in our lives or what we can do to make sure that our energy is not dragged down by them. If this person is a friend or someone we are in a relationship with, this will be a sign to let them go and move on or risk being held back by them.

If the people affecting us are members of our family or co-workers that on some level we have to have contact with, we have to learn to set firm boundaries. Within these boundaries we can have some peace and harmony. These boundaries may be physical in that we have a space and time where they are not permitted to intrude. More often the boundaries will need to be emotional. Here we have to make it clear what is acceptable and unacceptable behaviour. For instance, if someone is always bringing in their anger and guilt and dumping it on us, we need to make it clear that we will not permit this. It is not done by having a fight or dumping back on them. I always tell people that they need to give no energy to other people's negative behaviour. Make it clear by withdrawing physically, emotionally and mentally and in the process showing them that their behaviour is unacceptable.

This tactic works brilliantly with children. They want our attention above all else, if the best way to get this is by being naughty or difficult, they will milk this for all they are worth. We can train our children by giving no energy to bad behaviour and making them face the consequences of their actions. It is also essential to give lots of positive energy to them at other times. Most parents give very little when their children are being good and plenty while they are misbehaving. If our children are bringing disharmony to our environment, it is essential that this be dealt with as soon as possible. There is also nothing worse than children that are always squabbling with each other. Again, boundaries and consequences need to be brought in so that peace can be established and we are not living in a war zone.

Ultimately, in order to feel good all the time, we have to have a high degree of inner peace and harmony. This can then be reflected outward and into the external environment. When both the inner and outer aspects resonate with the highest part of our being, we feel absolutely brilliant.

TIPS FOR HARMONISING YOUR ENVIRONMENT

1) Make sure your clutter is cleared.
2) Look at your physical environment. Does it make you feel good being in it? Look at what would be in your power to change or enhance.
3) What colours work for you? Look at ways in which you can incorporate these colours both into your clothing and your decor. Tune in everyday to see what colour you need to wear to feel good and make your choices accordingly.
4) Look at how you can transform the rooms that you use. If the room colour is wrong or looks tatty, start by repainting. Look at the things and furniture in each room. Are any surplus to requirements? If so, pass them

on or throw them out. Make sure you have just the right amount of stuff in a room. Anything that does not resonate can be removed.

5) Bring fresh flowers and plants into your environment. Make sure they are in the right place by using trial and error.

6) Bring lovely smells and sounds into your homes.

7) Harmonise your workspace. Look at the changes that are needed to feel good there.

8) Do you have any inner conflicts? Isolate and identify the aspects within you that either go against what you want or are constantly fighting each other.

9) Are there people in your life that bring disharmony into your space. Do you need to let them go? What physical or emotional boundaries can you set to prevent them from bringing you down?

10) This is an ongoing process. As you change so will your environment. Keep refining and raising the energy levels around you.

KEY NINE
BE KIND

"You can know yourself to be kind, but unless you do someone a kindness, you have nothing but an idea about yourself"

BE KIND

Kindness is a hugely underrated quality and this is a shame because the world is badly in need of more of it. For the younger generation coming up, it isn't cool to be kind. There is peer pressure to put on a tough, hard exterior, the belief being that if we are too soft, we won't be able to survive in this difficult world. People who are kind are used and walked all over and treated as a mug.

We have also become very cynical and will often suspect the motives of anyone who is doing something nice without being asked or paid for it. We have all heard stories of con men and women who take advantage of vulnerable people by being kind to them. We are also aware that paedophiles will groom children by giving them things and doing nice things for them. Once they are hooked into this, the abuse will start and the child feels obligated to the abuser. We can see that on some levels we are right to be wary but we should not to let this be a reason not to practice kindness within our own lives.

Kindness works in two different ways. Kindness to others and being kind to ourselves. I will focus first of all on external kindness. I must stress here that what I am referring to here is unconditional kindness. There are many things that masquerade as kindness and are actually very different in their energy vibration. These will be things like control, manipulation and martyrdom. With control, we may use kindness as a hook to get someone on side. They may then become dependent on what we do for them, we can then control them by withdrawing the kindness anytime they do not do what we want. They very soon learn to dance to our tune and this is a very destructive and unhealthy pattern. The fact is that there is no genuine kindness at play within control. It is simply a means to an end.

Manipulation is often behind the kind acts of people and once again, it does not feel good. We might be kind or do nice things because we want people to like us. We try and make them feel as if they owe us for our kindness. It is like the unpopular child who gives sweets to the other children at school in order to try and buy friends. This will almost always backfire and create more bad feeling. Some people will keep an internal tally of what they do for others and almost see it as a debt building up. They may plan to call in the debt at a later date or like to feel powerful or superior to the people that they give to. We never feel very good around a manipulator and may even resent being made to feel beholden to them. We may not even want the things they do or give us.

Martyrs are another aspect of what I call negative kindness. A martyr will do or give seemingly at the expense of themselves and then let us know how deprived they are. For instance, if someone insisted on lending or giving us some money and then kept letting us know all the things they couldn't have because of it. We feel bad and we cannot enjoy the gift or the loan as a consequence. Martyrs get their kicks from making people know how great their sacrifice is.

People-pleasing is another negative kindness pattern. People-pleasers will usually have a great deal of low self-esteem and guilt and try to make themselves feel better by doing and giving to everyone. This is another way that trying to feel good backfires. People tend to take advantage of us and give back very little for what we do. We end up feeling used, abused and resentful. This is not a very satisfactory way of trying to feel good and needs to be changed.

Unconditional kindness is a very different kettle of fish. We expect nothing back in return for what we do, say or give. We cannot therefore be disappointed if we do not get a specific response. When we do get a very positive return on it, it is a huge bonus and will greatly raise our feel good quotient but it is the satisfaction of the initial act that makes us feel-good.

At its most basic level, unconditional kindness is something we do daily in how we treat people. When we are open, nice and friendly to everyone we encounter, we leave a bit of positivity behind with them. They feel better for having connected with us and so do we. In some ways this is old fashioned good manners: we say please and thank you and ask after their health.

Once we have this basic level running on a constant basis, we can go to a higher level. This involves doing a bit more. It doesn't need to cost anything in terms of time, energy or money. Spontaneity will be an important aspect of this. When we are awake and in the moment, we can see the opportunities for kindness as they present themselves. It may be helping an old lady with her bags or giving someone a lift who is waiting at a bus stop in the rain. It may be complimenting someone or entertaining a fractious child in a supermarket queue. The possibilities are endless and there will be many ways that we can achieve this. These acts of kindness are often to strangers and there can be no agenda because we do not plan to see them again. I know that when strangers have helped me in the past, I have felt brilliant. Many years ago, I arrived back from holiday to find that my car had two flat tyres. As I burst into tears in the street, a man stopped to help. He took both tyres to be mended and then changed them and would not even let me pay for the costs he incurred. I never saw him again but to this day I am still grateful for his unconditional kindness.

We can also up our kindness levels to family and friends that we have in our lives. We could plan a treat or surprise, send flowers to people for no particular reason or send a card to tell someone how much we appreciate them. We must make sure there are no expectations or agenda behind what we do. This is also an area in which we can use our creativity, both in the inspiration and in the way that we do it.

If we want to take our kindness to the next level, we could try anonymous giving. This way we know we are not looking to get anything back other than our own satisfaction. Here, it could be putting some cash in an envelope and posting it in the door of someone we know to be struggling. It could be doing the weeding or lawn for someone while they are out. It may be leaving some flowers or a plant for someone. You could always sign it from a guardian angel so they do not think they are being stalked. If we have a book that inspires us, we could give it anonymously to someone who might benefit from it. Again, the list is endless. We can also take great pleasure in planning these acts and imagining their reactions.

There was a lovely movement a few years ago called "Random Acts of Kindness." People were encouraged to practice unconditional giving. There were many touching stories that came out of this. Someone paid the toll for the ten cars behind them. The drivers of these cars didn't even see or know the donor but felt very good at being the recipient of the goodwill. The more creative we can be, the greater the impact.

We can also see the ripple effect working here. When we make people feel good by our kindness, they pass it on and the energy levels in the world and the feel good factor will lift on a global level. There is a film called "Pay it Forward" where a boy, as part of a school project devises a plan to do active things to help people. Instead of getting anything back, he tells them to pay it forward and get the people they pass it onto to do the same. A journalist hears of this and traces the ripple effect back until he finds the boy and the concept behind it. Something as simple as this can make a huge difference in the world.

Even a smile can be very powerful. I know that the times when I have caught a stranger's eyes and instead of looking away in embarrassment, I held their gaze and smiled and got a smile back in return, the effect has been amazing. In those few moments of wordless communication, we touch something deep within ourselves and in the other person. It does take courage to make this connection but well worth it when we do.

There is one proviso that we need to make in our unconditional kindness and that is that we do not set up expectations or dependency. This should never become a duty or obligation. It needs to be very much on our terms because we want to do it and we enjoy it. When someone is very needy and we appear to be providing what they need, this sets up a dependency. They then look to us to fulfil what they need. If we pull back on this as we inevitably have to as we have nothing left to give, they can get very angry and nasty despite all that we have already done. This pattern needs to be avoided at all costs. Our kindness needs to be empowering and the more we can vary it in terms of what we do and who we do it to, the better.

The objectives in our unconditional kindness are to make us feel good, the recipient of the kindness to feel good and to raise the positive energy quotient in the world as a whole. If what we do does not fulfil these three objectives, we need to look again at what we do or how we do it. Kindness will help to renew our and other's faith in human nature in this very negative world.

Being kind to ourselves will for many of us be a more challenging prospect than giving kindness to others. It never ceases to amaze me how nasty we are to ourselves. Most of this self-destructive behaviour is kept inside or is done behind closed doors. There is often a great deal of shame attached to this. We rarely see the extent to which many people dislike and abuse themselves.

There are many different ways in which we have to learn to be kind to ourselves. First, we need to become aware of how we talk to ourselves. Are we harsh, critical or abusive or do we give praise or encouragement to ourselves. I have often observed that if we have had a difficult childhood where one or both parents were unsupportive or abusive, when we remove ourselves from their influence, we take over the role of abuser. We have two separate aspects in our adult and child selves. The adult will harangue and criticise the child, telling it that it is useless and stupid. If we were accustomed to being blamed for everything in childhood, we will continue to blame ourselves as adults. I often come across people who find a way of taking the blame for things they are not even involved in. It is not just the things that we say to ourselves, it is the tone in which we say it. If it is not loving and nurturing, then we need to consciously make reparation in this area.

How we treat ourselves will be a habit and pattern that we might not even be aware of. If we have always done it, it will seem normal. Sometimes in our unkindness to ourselves, it is not so much what we do to ourselves but what we allow other people to do to us. The fact is that we teach people how to treat us and we have to take responsibility for this and not be a helpless victim. We show people how to treat us by setting boundaries. When they do or say something that steps over the line, we show or tell them so. Very soon they learn how far they can go with us and treat us accordingly. If we want to know how kind we are being to ourselves, we have only to look at how kind others are to us and measure it. We will also see how we are doing when we change our patterns and people behave differently to us. We do not need to be around people who treat us badly.

Our self-esteem will be very much linked with how we treat ourselves and how we let others treat us. We need to start consciously raising our self-esteem by being nice and actively doing things that will support us and not destroy us.

This step to feeling good is key because if we are not willing to be kind to ourselves, then we will not do the things needed in order to raise our feel good levels. If we are finding that we are resistant to making the necessary changes in our homes and lives to feel better, we may need to look at why we believe that we don't deserve to live the best possible life that we can. It may be issues from childhood that are getting in the way and these need to be addressed.

We also need to be kind to ourselves in terms of what we do and put into our bodies. This is one of the main ways in which we abuse ourselves. Do we smoke, drink to excess or take drugs? Do we put nutritious foods into our bodies or live on foods that provide little or no nutrition and set up unhealthy addictions and dependency? Do we exercise and tone up our bodies or is it just too much effort?

Once again, we are looking to raise our energy levels but this is on a very physical level. When we put too much sugar or refined foods into our bodies, they do not give us a good level of energy other than in the short term. They can even be quite depressive. When we are not getting good quality energy to spend in our lives, we will be depleted and exhausted.

Energy begets energy. When we do some exercise or activity, we may be expending energy but we also seem to have more at the end of the session. Exercise should never be a chore. We have to choose the things that suit us and our lifestyle. If we are not the types to enjoy the gym or any competitive sport, we could take up something like walking, golf or dancing. Exercise has to be put into our lives in an easy, enjoyable way or we will never keep it up. When we exercise, we release what are known as feel-good hormones. We will often feel great after our activity.

We need to take note of the ways in which we are not kind to our physical bodies. We will not be able to feel good if we are abusing our bodies and we will have to instigate some changes. This is particularly necessary if smoking or drugs is involved. This is nothing short of a slow suicide and total self-destruction.

One principle that I adhere to is "Do unto others as you would be done by." This works as a good guide. How would we feel if someone did or said something to us. If it makes us feel good, then this is a good thing to do for others. We can then extend it to ourselves and give it to us. This at least is in our total control and power and helps us to feel good.

TIPS FOR BEING KIND

1) Look at your kindness patterns. What do you do and give to others on a daily basis?

2) Is there an agenda behind what you do? What are you looking to get back in return? Do you use kindness as part of control, manipulation, martyrdom or people pleasing? These are all very negative patterns and will often create bad feeling on both sides. Look at changing these patterns.

3) Be aware of being open, warm, friendly, polite and nice on a daily basis.

4) Be spontaneous and in the moment and look out for the opportunities to be kind as they present themselves. Have no expectations of any gratitude or return on your kindness, only the satisfaction of having done it.

5) Be creative and look for ways in which you can practice anonymous or random acts of kindness. Enjoy the process and do not even look for the gratification of knowing or seeing their reaction.

6) See if you can set up a ripple effect of kindness. Encourage others to pass on the goodwill rather than look for it to come back to you. You could even print up a pass it on instruction and include this in any random acts of kindness.

7) Try everyday to catch a stranger's eye and smile. It could be while waiting at a traffic lights or in a shop. This is particularly satisfying with children.

8) Make sure you do not let anyone get dependent on or expect your kindness, do it at your discretion and not because they are asking for it.

9) Look at how kind you are to yourself. Do you mentally beat yourself up all the time? What tone of voice do you use on yourself? Take an hour when you simply observe your inner head talk and interaction with yourself. What do you notice? Actively try to lighten up in your treatment of yourself. Be kind and encouraging and not abusive. Nurture and support the child inside, who is crying out for kindness. Catch yourself when you are being nasty and change both the words and the tone.

10) Set boundaries for people and teach them how to treat you with kindness and respect.

11) Look at how you treat your body. Do you put toxic substances into it? Do you eat fresh nutritious foods or ones that are sweet or refined. Vow to make changes here. Put energy giving substances into your body and not destructive ones.

12) What exercise do you take? Do you always mean to do more but never get round to it? Can you make some of your fun or creative activities have a physical element to it like dancing or gardening? Start to increase your exercise and feel good about your body.

13) Remember to do unto others as you would be done by.

KEY TEN
HAVE FUN

"If it isn't fun, why do it?"

HAVE FUN

Some of our best feel good moments occur when we are having fun. My personal motto is "if it isn't fun, don't do it." Fun will lift our mood and raise our energy vibration. What constitutes fun is going to vary hugely from person to person. I would not find climbing a mountain fun, but many people do. To each their own.

Fun and happiness work in a very similar way. Our desire for happiness is one of the main motivating forces we have and yet we tend to go the wrong way about attaining it. We are often very passive about it and look for people, situations or things to make us happy. The fact is that happiness is a choice and decision that we make. We then bring that happiness into all areas of life. This puts our happiness firmly in our own power and control. It is exactly the same with fun, we do not look to people or activities to bring us fun, we put fun into everything that we do.

Much of what we have to do is going to be mundane or routine. It may be hard to see how we can make even those things fun. Fun is an attitude of mind. We can put our favourite music on while washing the kitchen floor or watch a funny DVD while doing the ironing.

Fun comes from the child aspect of ourselves and it is important to develop this side of ourselves. I always see that there are two distinct parts of the inner child. There is the happy child and the damaged child. These could not be more different from each other. The happy child personifies our ideal perception of how a child ought to be. It is full of joy, imagination, creativity, fun and laughter. It sees life as one big adventure and yet feels secure, loved and nurtured. In contrast the damaged child will have experienced first hand a reality very different from this. It may have experienced abuse, neglect, an absence of love and inconsistent boundaries. There may have been traumatic things that happened like the loss of a parent or sibling or parents splitting up that contributed to the damage.

When we try to have fun and access the damaged child and all its fear, anger and pain, we are going to avoid it. This is the pattern of the workaholic. They shy away from anything that will put them in touch with the child and emotions. This will include things like holidays, spending time with their children and playing games. Workaholics may play computer games or do competitive sports because they do not access the child aspect.

In order to bring our happy child into our life, play and fun, we have to heal and let go the damage of childhood. This very much comes into letting the past go. If we have had a particularly difficult time as a child, we might even have to learn to have fun. This may take time and we have to get used to the idea of doing things for sheer enjoyment. Creativity will often have a big part to play in this.

Laughter will play a huge part in our having fun. It is impossible to feel bad when we are laughing. Laughter will raise our energy vibration and transmute even the most dense fear energy. When we are children, we laugh all the time. It is very much a part of how we play and what we do. As we get older the degree to which we laugh diminishes hugely. Some people find very little to laugh about when they are stuck in struggle and survival. We have to make an active choice to bring laughter into our lives.

A sense of humour is probably the most important quality that I look for in the people I choose to spend my time with. I want to have a good laugh even when we are dealing with difficult subjects. I have numerous nephews and nieces and I love being with them because they are so funny. Their wit and humour are always there and I always feel good after being in their company.

Laughter has been found to be brilliant medicine. Some people even claim that it has cured them of serious illnesses like cancer. Others have said that it has got them through the bad times and family illnesses. We have to look for and find the laughter and humour within us and not just passively wait for it to come to us. We can watch programmes or films that make us laugh or read books that come into that genre. We also need to make sure we spend time with people who have a similar sense of humour to ourselves.

Fun and laughter need to be brought into absolutely every area of life. It is not just something we do at the end of the day if we have the time and energy. Most people spend the majority of time at work so it is imperative that it be fun. People who have a good laugh with plenty of witty banter at work, will look forward to the time they spend in the workplace instead of dreading it. It also helps if there is a social side to our work where we can connect with our work mates in a light and pleasurable way.

It is essential that we bring fun and laughter into our relationships. This alone can be enough to keep it strong and sustain us through the difficult patches. When we laugh at the same things or are in a playful mode with each other, we open ourselves up and allow our partners into a very deep part of us. Relationships that do not have the benefit of any fun or laughter will often be doomed. It does take effort and imagination to keep bringing this in. It may be having in jokes that we keep reinforcing or playing games. This is also an important aspect of keeping our sex lives alive, healthy and interesting.

'Families that play together, stay together,' as the saying goes. I have noticed that the families that are close are usually full of fun and laughter. They want to get together because they have a good time when they do. Children give us a wonderful opportunity to connect with the playful, fun side of ourselves. I think it is a huge shame when parents do not interact and play with their children at this level.

If fun is not a natural part of our lives then we need to look for ways to bring it in to a greater degree. We can bring it into all the things that we do but we can also find the things that we enjoy and schedule them into our lives. Everyone is going to be different, so we have to be clear as to what constitutes fun for us. Do we enjoy being with like-minded people in either a social or learning environment? Do we like doing things like singing, dancing or doing a craft or creative activities? It is always better if we can do this with other people as this gives an added dimension to the fun. Do we enjoy having friends or family round to our homes or going to the theatre or art galleries? Whatever it is that brings fun into our lives, it needs to be made a priority for us. A fun activity will be a very positive investment and will usually give us back far more energy than we have had to invest into it. For this reason alone it is well worth making the effort to have it as a key part of our lives.

Fun and laughter will lighten up any situation that we find ourselves in and the people who bring these elements to us are always going to be in great demand. It is also perfectly possible for us to entertain and bring fun and laughter in when we are on our own. We can see the fun and funny side of things at all times.

TIPS FOR HAVING FUN

1) Look at what your fun quotient is. Is it something that is an integral part of your life or something that you only experience occasionally?
2) Look at your patterns with fun. Are you passive and wait for others to bring it to you or do you initiate it? Are you struck in survival and find it hard to have fun? Do you suffer from depression and struggle to see the lighter side of life?
3) Do you have a good connection with your inner child? When it emerges, are you in touch with the damaged or happy child? Does it feel negative or positive?
4) Make a huge effort to keep clearing and healing the damaged child and notice how much more often the happy child is able to emerge.
5) How often do you laugh? Do you actively look to see the funny side of things? Make an effort to laugh more.
6) Look at the different areas of your life and notice how much fun and laughter you bring into them.
7) How much fun do you have at work? Are you with people who are fun and that you can socialise with? If not, what can you do to change this? You may need to be the one to create it.
8) In your relationships, do you prioritise fun into what you do and how you connect?
9) Do you choose to have friends and people around you who are light, fun and make you laugh? If not it would be worth broadening your circle of friends or letting anyone go who does not resonate with you.
10) Do you have children around you? Take every opportunity to connect with them and let the child in you out to play, they will love it and so will you.

11) Do you connect with your extended family? Make sure that times when you are together are light and fun, so that everyone will make the effort to get together more often.

12) What activities would bring more fun into your life? Make a list. Start to put out feelers as to where and how you could enjoy these things more.

13) Prioritise and schedule fun into your life. Look at how you could bring it into the mundane and boring areas of your life. See if anyone or anything is blocking you from having more fun and see what you can do to change it.

14) Inject joy, fun and laughter into every part of your being and your life.

KEY ELEVEN
TAKE TIME FOR YOURSELF

*The most important relationship
is the one that we have
with ourselves.*

TAKE TIME FOR YOURSELF

For many people, taking time for themselves is a luxury that they feel they can ill-afford but in reality it is essential. We are in a relationship with ourselves and as with any relationship, it will only be a success if we are willing to invest time and energy into it.

We are very complex beings with many different aspects that contribute to the whole person that we are. There is the adult and the child aspect that I have already referred to in this book. Added to these is the spirit, soul or higher self. The adult, child and spirit are what I call the trinity. This is a similar dynamic to what is known in the Christian religion as the Holy Trinity, the Father, Son and Holy Ghost. For us to be living an optimal existence, it is essential that the aspects of the trinity are working in harmony. The spirit gives us love, nurture, guidance, wisdom, inspiration and support. The adult is the practical, logical aspect that gets things done. It tends to work with the mind and is the thinker and doer. The child works with emotions and brings creativity, imagination, joy, fun, laughter and play into our lives.

All of these three sides to us are necessary if we want to feel good and to achieve our highest purpose. They also need to be in balance, with each aware of the role that they play. Most people are primarily working with their adult selves. This is why the majority are stuck in struggle and survival. As the adult works with the mind, it is associated with the ego, which feeds us fear through our thoughts. These are what I call "what ifs…" If we have shut out our spirit, we will not hear the guidance that tells us where to go and what to do to be on our paths. If we go into a state of emotional shutdown, we cut off from the child aspect of ourselves and in the process detach from the joy, fun and creativity. We also access our spirit through the emotions. Feelings are the language of the soul.

To get our trinity working optimally takes time and space. We have to make sure that the channels of information are open and being received. Any wasted investment of time, energy or money are going to occur because our adult is acting unilaterally, without the guidance from the higher self. Any lack of joy is going to be because we are not bringing the child into the equation.

Our intuition is the single most important tool that we have at our disposal. We cannot fail to have an amazing, wonderful life if we listen to and act upon our intuition. There will always be negative consequences to our overriding our intuition. The intuition is the hot line to the higher self and must be allowed to work at all times.

Taking time for ourselves is essential because this is when we can connect and build up a relationship with the intuition. We need to ask questions of our higher selves and listen for the answers when they arrive. If we do not give ourselves the space for this, we will miss the vital information when it comes. We have to learn to develop the intuition by tuning into it. It is a very subtle energy and may require some fine tuning. We cannot do this in the hustle and bustle of everyday life or when there are people around. Part of each day needs to be given to this tuning in process.

We also need the time and space to connect and develop the child aspect of ourselves. Part of this is fulfilling the needs of the child. We tend to look to other people to do this for us and it can put too high a burden on friends, family and partners. They will often back off under the burden of our needs. If our adult selves takes on the responsibility of fulfilling the needs of the child, it is in our own control and we do not need to exert any control over others to get our needs met. When we take time to tune into the child, we can also heal any damage from the past that it may have sustained. When we do this, we bring more of the happy child to the surface.

Taking time for ourselves is not about finding space for our doing, it is about providing room for our being, which is far more important. Our being is very much in the moment and aware. It will be able to see both the opportunities and the blocks when they present themselves. Within our being is love, abundance, joy and all the good things of life. If we are not in touch with it, we will miss out on all this bounty.

Taking time for ourselves is a very necessary part of our self-discovery. We often talk about "finding ourselves" or finding out who we are. I think that a better way of doing this is deciding who we want to be. In order to do this, we have to first discover who we do not want to be and release these aspects of ourselves. As I said, I work a great deal with sub-personalities. Simply by identifying the destructive personalities, we can dismantle the negative aspects and build on their strengths so that they work for us and not against us. If we have very negative, dominant sub-personalities, it is imperative that they are dealt with before they sabotage or destroy us.

We also need to take time for ourselves in order to process the things that happen to us on a daily basis. If we do not do this, we will get a backlog that will slow our energy and momentum down. We will feel tired and sluggish and unable to perform optimally. The processing that I am referring to here is on many levels. First of all we have to clear and express any emotions that arise. It might be anger with a partner, child or boss or pain at any perceived slight or rejection. We may feel guilt for not visiting a relative or for not doing what we said we would. These will often be very little things but if allowed to fester can grow into far bigger issues. Part of our processing is also about assimilating what works and what doesn't. This is an essential aspect of our growth and learning and if we do not take the time, the opportunity will be lost. Mistakes are only there to show us what does not work and we are simply meant to learn from them, not to beat ourselves up for them. Equally, when we discover what does work we want to cement and solidify it by analysing what the components were that produced the results that we wanted. It takes time and space to be able to do this processing and will prove to be a very productive investment.

One of the best ways to take time for ourselves is by spending time in nature. I have already established all the benefits that trees, plants and flowers bring to us. By actively putting ourselves in that environment, we raise our energy, process our negative emotions and get the benefits of fresh air. I walk my dog in nature every day and it is hugely beneficial for me. If this is not practical or possible, time in a garden or park will be helpful. If you live in a city, plan breaks out into nature whenever you can and top up your batteries to see you through. This is an active thing and needs to be put into your routine or planned in advance. It is easy to get stuck in a rut and allow this to lapse. Our holidays should also be a time to have a change of scene, recharge and take some time and space in nature.

Many people find that doing something like meditation, yoga or t'ai chi helps them to connect with their inner selves and is very beneficial on many levels. This is something that needs to be done on a regular basis and become part of our routines and life.

It is important to see how, where and when we want to take time for ourselves and make sure it becomes a priority rather than just something we fit in after everything else has been done. We could do things like have a long, hot scented bath. We could book in for a massage or facial. We could go for a walk or sit in the garden. When we are taking time for ourselves, it is very helpful to become aware of our breathing. It is the breath that will get in touch with our inspiration and inner knowing. The word "inspire" actually means to breathe in. I also find that in processing negative emotions or patterns, the easiest way to do this is to simply breathe out. When we see something very beautiful like a sunset or a moonlit sky, we often drink them in by breathing in. This helps us to feel it as well as see it. Just increasing the depth and fullness of our breathing can help to dispel fear and put the body in a calm, relaxed state.

We can also use things to enhance the time we spend with ourselves. It could be something like lighting candles, putting on gentle, relaxing music or having a drink. In a way we need to learn to romance ourselves in order to get the most out of the relationship that we have with ourselves. We can look at what we would like or expect from a partner in the romance line. These are the things that we need to give ourselves.

TIPS FOR TAKING TIME FOR YOURSELF

1) Look at the state of the relationship that you have with yourself. Is it loving and kind or are you tough and abusive to yourself? How much time do you devote to developing this relationship?

2) Are you in touch with and connected to your inner child? Make sure that you are aware of the needs of that child and make it a priority to fulfil them, rather than looking to others to do so. These needs may be things

like praise, reassurance, love, stimulation, expression of emotions or security. See your adult and child selves being very distinct from each other. Check in regularly with your inner child and keep on healing any baggage from the past so that your happy child can emerge.

3) Make the connection with your higher self or soul. This can be done through intuition. Make sure that you connect daily with your intuition and before making any major decisions, check in with it. Learn how your intuition gets through to you. It may be through feelings, a vision, a voice, dreams or symbols and signposts or it may be a mixture of all of these. Keep building a stronger relationship with your intuition. This is your best friend!

4) Take time to look at yourself and your personality. This will often be shown by how you react in different situations. What parts of yourself do you like or dislike? These will probably be some of your sub-personalities. You can become the person you most want to be by removing the negative or destructive sub-personalities. These will be things like the control freak, the tyrant, the victim, the saboteur, the addict or the rebel. Tere are processes that can be done to clear and diffuse these.

5) Take time every day to process and work on what has gone on that day. It may be releasing safely any emotions that have surfaced. It may also be looking at your actions and acknowledging which ones worked and which ones didn't. Don't let yourself get too behind in your processing or you will get bogged down in the backlog.

6) Take time for yourself in nature as often as you can. If you do not have access to the countryside, a garden or park will suffice. You will notice how much better you feel even with as little as ten minutes a day.

7) Look at the things you could do to enhance your relationship with yourself. Be romantic. Whatever you would love your partner to do or give you, give to yourself. Make the time you spend with yourself special.

8) Look at taking up things like meditation, yoga or t'ai chi to enhance your connection with yourself.

9) Take the time to be inspired. Use the breath to access the inspiration and make sure you put it into action and do not let it just remain as an idea.

10) Notice how much your feel good factor increases when you improve your relationship with yourself.

KEY TWELVE
GRATITUDE

When we express and feel gratitude
for even the smallest insight, gift or
flower, we open the way to receive the
full magnificence of the Universe.

GRATITUDE

In all the other keys to feeling good, I have either advocated letting go or bringing in various physical or emotional things. In this final step, I am simply advising that we do not need to do or change anything other than our attitudes or our minds. Gratitude allows us to find the feel-good factor in what we have and are right now, rather than be and have the things we think we want to make us feel good.

We are so powerful that we create our own reality. We partly do this by how we choose to perceive a person or situation. Our perception of them creates what they become for us, regardless of the reality of the situation. We cannot control people or situations but we can control our attitude to them. They then become what we want them to be. In reality most things are neutral, they just are. It is when we put either a positive or negative emotional charge onto things that they assume these roles in our lives.

Gratitude is one way that we can put a positive charge onto the things and people around us. It sees only the good and the benefits around us. It is an obvious fact that optimists feel better about themselves and life than pessimists. We can choose to be optimists, we simply have to look for the good in everything we do and see. It will always be there even in the most difficult or tragic of circumstances.

Looking for and finding the gift in everything needs to become a natural part of our lives. As human beings our tendency is to dwell on the negative. If ten good things happen to us and one bad thing occurs, we will often let the one bad thing cancel out the good. We dwell on it and let it lower our energy vibration. The fact is that whatever we put our energy focus and attention on will expand and magnify. The amount we invest in it will determine the degree to which we feel the positive or negative energy. If we are constantly putting our focus onto the negative, then we will feel bad all the time. The only thing we need to take from a negative situation is the lesson and gift that it was there to impart. It might be what not to do next time or it might involve removing ourselves from something that is destructive to us.

Gratitude is essential because it helps us to appreciate and be happy with what we have right now. It is about wanting what we have got rather than getting what we want. Gratitude is also a brilliant way of keeping us in the present because we are not constantly looking forward to getting what we think we want.

Life is in a constant state of flux and movement. As long as we are going with the flow, things will continue to change. Our gratitude therefore has to change with it. It becomes a wonderful way of seeing and acknowledging our progress on a daily basis. It also raises the feel good factor. We can use this as a barometer. If we are not constantly finding new things to be grateful for, then this will be an indication that we are stuck or blocked and something needs to be done to dislodge us. This is in itself a gift.

We also need to look for a win for everyone involved in a situation. So often we find ourselves in a win/lose position. With a bit of fine tuning we can make sure that we are in a win/win situation. This may involve changing our attitudes to what constitutes loss. We may need to remove a negative emotional charge that we have projected onto the thing before we are able to put a positive one on it. The negative perspective is there because of how we chose to perceive the situation at the time. If we allow ourselves to perceive the same situation in a positive light, we can change the polarity of the charge and only see the good in it. If we created the original feelings, thoughts and beliefs, we can dismantle that creation and recreate it in a way that serves us and makes us feel good and not bad.

It is also very helpful when we can be happy for the good fortune of others. There is a particularly destructive trait within the human condition, whereby we resent it when people have things or succeed in life where we have not. Some people actively dislike others who have what they want. When we do this, we will in effect block those things from coming to us. We will have put a negative charge on the success, house, car, relationship or fame and this will then repel them from coming into our lives. Many people tell me of the negative response they got when something really good happened to them in their lives. We have to look at it that we are better off finding out who our genuine friends and supporters are and letting the rest go. We do not want people in our lives who have a vested interest in keeping us small or using and abusing our energy. We need to notice when we feel jealous or resentful that others have gained either materially or in terms of their success. We can then make a concerted effort to be happy for them. This will then allow us to have the same good fortune come into our own lives.

We can also use gratitude as a means of programming what we want into our lives. We manifest what we want for the most part unconsciously. All our inner thoughts, beliefs and feelings will contribute to what we end up creating. We usually make the mistake of putting our wishes and wants into the future. The unconscious mind is very literal and if we put something out into the future, this is where it will stay. Tomorrow never comes! By using gratitude, we can thank our inner selves for what we don't yet have. Being as literal as it is, it will do its damnedest to give us what we have already thanked it for. I will often use this technique at the beginning of a day or a journey. I will put out thanks that everything happens smoothly and in its perfect time and place. Before a journey I give thanks for getting me to my destination safely and at the perfect time. It is very powerful to put thanks into our programming for the smallest of things. One time I was doing a journey into London in rush hour and I was slightly late leaving so I gave thanks for getting me there at the particular, desired time. As it happened there was virtually no traffic and as I was getting near my destination, I was about ten minutes in advance of the programmed time. I had been to this place many times and knew the route well but took a wrong turning and got lost. I turned up at my destination at the exact minute that I had programmed. So literal was my inner self that when it realised I would be early, it had to make a detour. I now put into the programming that I get there at the most desirable time.

I firmly believe that the more grateful we are, the more we are given. The Universe responds positively to us and sends back the good will. We know ourselves that when we give gifts or do things for people and we do not receive any thanks or gratitude, we are disinclined to do or give anything in future. In contrast to this, when we get genuine gratitude back for what we do or give, we feel good. We then want to keep on giving more in order to perpetuate the feel good factor. Do not take anything for granted.

Gratitude is a wonderful way of taking stock or inventory of our lives. If we notice all the positives and things we have to be grateful for, we reinforce them. It also helps us to see what we are not so grateful for, in effect the deadwood that we are carrying. This then gives us an opportunity to clear it out. Most of us are not aware of the destructive elements in our lives because we do not choose to see them. Gratitude can play a huge part in paring our lives down to having only things that work well for us and putting positive elements in.

Gratitude is something that needs to be done on a daily or regular basis. First thing in the morning and last things at night are the best times. In the morning we are looking at the day ahead and programming it with gratitude. At the end of the day we are taking stock of the gains made, the lessons learned and the gifts given. By putting gratitude into these things, we will expand them and the positivity involved.

TIPS FOR BRINGING IN GRATITUDE

1) Look at the people, situations and factors in your life and notice the degree to which you put a negative charge on them. Do you see the wrong rather than what is right with them?
2) For each person or thing, look at how you chose to perceive them in the past. Take off any negative charges put on them and look for and find the positives. The people who give you the most grief are often your best teachers. Difficult situations will often occur to make you move on or question yourself and your life. You might be being shown how you have created what you don't want so that you can begin to create what you do.
3) Find the gift in everything that occurs in your life.
4) Keep looking for solutions until you create a win for both yourself and others involved in the situation. It will be there but you may need to change your perception of what constitutes a win.
5) Use gratitude to programme your day ahead or any difficult situation that is looming. Make sure you phrase it in the present tense. It might be

something like saying "Thank you for providing the best possible outcome for this situation for all involved", if you have a tricky meeting ahead. Or, "thank you for getting me to my destination safely and in perfect time", if you are going on a journey.

6) Regularly use gratitude to take an inventory of your life. All the things you can find to be grateful for are playing a positive role in your life. If you cannot see any reason for gratitude in anything or anyone, then it is time to clear them out.

7) Rejoice and be grateful for the good fortune of others and in the process increase your own chances of attracting it. This must be genuine and not just paying lip service to it for your own gain. If this is a problem for you, you need to look for the underlying causes of this issue.

8) Get into the habit of bringing in gratitude on a daily basis. It will only take moments of your time. Some people find it helpful to write it down and have a gratitude diary. Try to find at least five things to be grateful for. Go to sleep with these positives in the forefront of your mind. Do not let any negative situations cancel out the good.

FINAL NOTE

This is my thirteenth book completed and I have enjoyed it more than any other book that I have written. One of the main reasons for this is that I have been putting into practice all the steps as they have been formulated. I can honestly say that everything in my life has improved as a result. My energy levels and productivity have doubled if not tripled. I have always tended to be quite passive and reactive and now I find that this has changed and I am very proactive. Procrastination, which is one of the manifestations of fear, used to be my middle name, now I find I want to do everything in advance of any deadline and do not have the build up of pressure and resistance that used to be there. I am seeing my life with far less limitation. Things that I would not have dreamt of tackling in the past now seem to be a distinct probability. I do feel good, most of the time.

As with all of my books, this one has been given to me. I feel as if they come through me rather than from me. I certainly feel as if this book is a great gift to me and I trust that this can be extended to all those who read it.

The twelve steps are all things that are ongoing in our lives and consequently will keep on adding to the feel good factor. There may need to be a concerted effort in the early days to do things like clear clutter and to let the past go but after that it is simply about maintaining it and dealing with what comes up. Things like creativity, fun, kindness, gratitude and time for ourselves need to be incorporated into our everyday lives until they become a natural part of what we do. Remember, this is an active process, knowing it will not change anything. If we change nothing, nothing changes.

I wish each and everyone of you a life filled with joy, fulfilment, abundance, fun and love.

LIZ ADAMSON

FINAL PAGE

Liz Adamson is available for talks, workshops and intensive one to one sessions.
Contact. Liz Adamson at Flat 3, Hamptons, Hadlow, Tonbridge, Kent. UK. TN11 9SR. Tel (UK) 01732-810430.
Email: liz@edenbook.co.uk
Website: www.lizadamson.co.uk

Also available by Liz Adamson:

The 12 Principles of Optimal Living	£7.95
Overcoming Sexual and Childhood Abuse.	£7.95
Overcoming Weight Issues	£7.95
Relationships, A Journey into Wholeness	£7.95
Abundance and Prosperity	£7.95

THE ULTIMATE GUIDES TO EMOTIONAL FREEDON

Releasing Anger	£4.95
Releasing Hurt and Sadness	£4.95
Releasing Fear	£4.95
Releasing Guilt	£4.95
Embracing Happiness	£4.95
Embracing Love	£4.95
The above titles are available on Audio CD	£9.95
CD—Subliminal Overcoming Weight Issues	£9.95
The Secrets of Optimal Living Insight Cards	£7.95

All these are available via the Website: www.lizadamson.co.uk

978-0-595-37316-1
0-595-37316-X

Printed in the United Kingdom
by Lightning Source UK Ltd.
108726UKS00002B/118-255